DON'T TRIP!

A Beginner-Friendly Guide to Foraging for Mushrooms the Safe Way

By
ANTHONY BARRETT

Copyright © 2023 by Anthony Barrett All Rights Reserved

All rights reserved. No part of this publication may be reproduced, stored or transmitted in any form or by any means, electronic, mechanical, photocopying, recording, scanning, or otherwise without written permission from the publisher. It is illegal to copy this book, post it to a website, or distribute it by any other means without permission.

Anthony Barrett asserts the moral right to be identified as the author of this work.

Anthony Barrett has no responsibility for the persistence or accuracy of URLs for external or third-party Internet Websites referred to in this publication and does not guarantee that any content on such Websites is, or will remain, accurate or appropriate.

Designations used by companies to distinguish their products are often claimed as trademarks. All brand names and product names used in this book and on its cover are trade names, service marks, trademarks and registered trademarks of their respective owners. The publishers and the book are not associated with any product or vendor mentioned in this book. None of the companies referenced within the book have endorsed the book.

The content within this book may not be reproduced, duplicated, or transmitted without direct written permission from the author or the publisher.

Under no circumstances will any blame or legal responsibility be held against the publisher, or author, for any damages, reparation, or monetary loss due to the information contained within this book, either directly or indirectly. The author of this book does not guarantee the accuracy of the information herein.

Legal Notice:

This book is copyright protected. It is only for personal use. You cannot amend, distribute, sell, use, quote, or paraphrase any part of the content within this book, without the consent of the author or publisher.

Disclaimer Notice:

Please note the information contained within this document is for educational and entertainment purposes only. All effort has been expended to present accurate, up-to-date, reliable, and complete information. No warranties of any kind are declared or implied. Readers acknowledge that the author is not engaged in the rendering of legal, financial, medical, or professional advice. The content within this book has been derived from various sources. Please consult a licensed professional before attempting any techniques outlined in this book.

By reading this document, the reader agrees that under no circumstances is the author responsible for any losses, direct or indirect, that are incurred as a result of the use of the information contained within this document, including, but not limited to, errors, omissions, or inaccuracies.

First edition

A Special Gift To Our Readers

Included with your purchase of this book is a free digital copy of our mindset survival guide 7 *Essential Habits of the Consummate Survivor: How Anyone Can Adopt a Survival Mindset and Refuse to be a Victim*. This invaluable manual will help prepare you to take on any situation and survive. From situational awareness, to avoiding or deescalating violent encounters, this book could save your life.

Follow the link below for your free eBook so we know which email to send it to.

Barrettsurvival.com

TABLE OF CONTENTS

Introduction xi

Chapter One: What's so Great About Mushrooms? 1

Chapter Two: A Brief (But Epic) History of Humans and Mushrooms 4
    Mushrooms as Medicine 5
    Foraging as a Way of Life 5
    Ancient and Modern Psychedelic Culture 6
    The Mycelial Roots of Halloween 7
    Magic Mushrooms in the New World 8

Chapter Three: Who Loves Mushrooms, Aside from You and Me? 9
    Mushrooms for the Future 9
    Fungi Actively Protect and Restore the Environment 10
    Mushrooms and the Climate 12

Chapter Four: What is a Mushroom, Anyway? 14
    The Feeding Habits of Mushrooms 14
    Four Types of Fungi that Produce Mushrooms 15
        Mycorrhizal Fungi 15
        Saprotrophic Fungi 16
        Parasitic Fungi 16
        Endophytic Fungi 16
    Mushroom Reproduction 17

Chapter Five: Mushroom Anatomy 18

   Agaric (Gilled) Mushrooms 20

      Identifying Species of Agaric Mushrooms 20

   Bolete Types 22

      Identifying Bolete-Type Mushrooms 23

   Spine Mushrooms 23

   Other Stipe-and-Cap Mushrooms 23

   Cup Mushrooms 23

   Coral/Fan-Like Fungi 23

   Polypore and Crust Fungi 24

   Puffballs and Earthballs 24

   Truffles and Truffle-Like Fungi 24

   Jellies 25

   A Few Other Non-Conformists 25

   Rules of Thumb 25

   Talk Like a Mushroom 26

Chapter Six: Field Guide to Common Edible Mushrooms 28

   Easy Pickings 28

   Giant Puffballs (Calvatia gigantea) 29

   Chicken of the Woods (Laetiporus species) 31

   Hen of the Woods (Grifola frondose) 32

   Dryad's Saddle (Polyporus squamosus) 34

   Hedgehog Mushrooms (Hydnum repandum) 35

   Beefsteak Fungus (Fistulina hepatica) 37

   For the Discerning Gourmand 38

   Chanterelles (Cantharellus genus) 38

   Morels (Morchella genus) 42

   King Boletes (Boletus edulis) 44

   Oyster Mushrooms (Pleurotus ostreatus) 46

   Black Trumpets (Cantharellaceae genus) 48

   Shaggy Manes (Coprinus comatus) 49

Lobster Mushrooms (Hypomyces lactifluorum) 51

Chapter Seven: Ferocious Fungi 53

Ten to Watch Out For..53

False Parasol (chlorophyllum molybdites) 54

Death Cap (Amanita phalloides)...55

Destroying Angel (Amanita virosa)...56

False Morel (Gyromitra genus)...57

Funeral Bell or Autumn Skullcap (Galerina marginata) 58

Fool's Webcap (Cortinarius orellanus) 59

Common Conecap or Duncecap (Conocybe genus) 60

Angel Wings (Pleurocybella porrigens) 61

Fly Agarics (Amanita muscaria & Amanita pantherine) 62

Deadly Dapperling (Lepiota brunneoincarnata) 63

How To Avoid Mushroom Poisoning 63

If You Suspect Mushroom Poisoning 64

Chapter Eight: Mushroom Medicine 65

Three Common Wild Mushrooms to Keep You Healthy 66

Chaga (Inonotus obliquus)..66

Maitake (Grifola frondosa) 68

Bear's Head (Hericium Americanum) 69

Proceed with Caution and Seek Professional Guidance..69

Chapter Nine: The Kaleidoscopic Killers 71

Foraging for Magic Mushrooms...71

What are Magic Mushrooms? 72

Are Magic Mushrooms Safe? 73

Legal Precautions for Foraging and Eating Magic Mushrooms 73

The Most Common Magic Mushrooms in North America 73

Liberty Caps (Psilocybe semilanceata) 74

Wavy Caps (Psilocybe cyanescens) 75

Flying Saucers (Psilocybe Azurescens) 76

Gold Caps or Cubes (Psilocybe Cubensis) 77

Magic Mushrooms in Psychotherapy 77

Chapter Ten: The Rare Rubies 79

Bioluminescent Mushrooms 79

Mushrooms that Bleed 80

Floral Mushrooms 80

Insectivores 81

Calling all Citizen Mycologists 81

Chapter Eleven: Before You Go Foraging 82

Know Where to Go 82

Bring What You Need 83

    Something to Put Them In 84

    Tools of the Trade 84

    The Paperwork 85

    Your Crew 86

    Standard Hiking Gear 86

Chapter Twelve: The Spotless Forager 87

Personal Safety 87

When to Pick It and When to Leave it Alone 88

Low-Impact Foraging 89

Laws and Regulations 89

Chapter Thirteen: Forward, Forager! 92

The best places to forage for wild edible mushrooms in the US 92

    Pacific Northwest 92

    North Central 93

    Midwest 93

    Northeast 94

    Southeast 94

    South Central 94

    Southwest 95

    Alaska 95

    Frequently Asked Questions about Mushroom Hunting 95

    Mushroom Foraging Checklist 97

Sharing Your Bounty 98

Conclusion 99

Bibliography 101

INTRODUCTION

My first backpacking trek through the Olympic Peninsula was full of surprises, not the least of which was spotting a pair of brightly colored floral head scarves bobbing along on the other side of a patch of devil's club under the Douglas fir canopy. I lingered on the trail, wondering if the two women were lost.

As I watched, it became apparent that these two grandmothers, who looked like they had stepped out of a bygone century, weren't in a hurry to get anywhere. Steadily moving toward the trail where I stood, they were so intent on scanning the thick, spongy litter on the forest floor that they didn't see me standing there until one of them almost bumped into me.

"Mushroom hunting?" I guessed. I had been told that the area had a reputation for excellent mushroom harvests.

The woman shook her head no, but her flashing blue eyes told me something different. The bulging paper sack she held in her hands made me wonder. I'd heard that mushroom hunters can be quite secretive when plying their trade so I decided not to pry.

As I continued walking, I stopped in a few places to lift the decaying leaves around rotting logs. Of the several types of mushrooms I saw – tall and white, shiny brown buttons, creamy ruffles, bright orange tendril-like growths – I wondered which mushrooms the two women were hunting and what they might taste like.

At the time I didn't know much about mushrooms beyond the fact that many are deadly, so I didn't risk picking any. Instead, I gathered fiddleheads and nettle leaves to garnish my dinner plate that night when I set up camp.

That night, I lay awake listening to the soft, distant hoot of a pair of owls calling to each other through the fog and wondered about the mushrooms I was missing out on.

When I emerged from the forest the next day, I recognized those same two scarves at a wide spot next to the road just before the nearest town. The women were sitting on the tailgate of an old pickup, a line of paper sacks stretched out between them. When I got closer, I saw that behind the sacks were flats of thick, bright orange funnels with gills going up the sides, as if the mushrooms had been turned inside out. Some of them were almost as big as my fist.

"Looks like you made a good haul!" I said.

The woman who had denied that she was mushroom hunting the day before smiled and nodded, with no hint of an apology for the lie. "And you? How much did you get?" Her accent was unmistakably Slavic.

I hated to admit it, but on this, my first backpacking trip in the Pacific Northwest, I had missed out on one of its greatest treasures. I humbly consider myself an expert outdoorsman with a ton of experience. The first book I authored, *Master the World of Edible Wild Plants*, has encouraged thousands of nature enthusiasts to get out into the wilderness and treat themselves to fresh, nutrient-packed foods that they will never find in a grocery store.

When it comes to mushrooms though, I've always known that it's vitally important to make sure you know what you're doing. Some common mushrooms that can easily pass for edible varieties to the untrained eye could kill you on the spot. I had wanted to learn about mushrooms for a while but hadn't yet made it a priority. After I had sauteed and eaten the mushrooms I bought that day, I was eager to make up for lost time.

Since then, I've learned that the mushrooms those women were foraging are called chanterelles. Hearty mushrooms with a mild fruity flavor and hints of pepper, chanterelles can be used as a substitute for meat, or you can add them to meat dishes to augment the flavor. Pairing them with venison and bacon are two of my favorite ways to eat chanterelles. Like many mushrooms, these beauties cannot be cultivated. They only grow in lush forest environments that are relatively undisturbed by human activity.

I've gone on to forage mushrooms from coast to coast in diverse mountain ranges and all kinds of forests. Whether I'm hunting large game in the mountains, fishing in lazy rivers, digging clams on the coast, or collecting wild vegetables in the hill country, knowing which mushrooms I can safely harvest from the vicinity has vastly enriched my adventures as well as my campfire recipes.

If you're like me, always looking for ways to deepen your connection with nature and become more self-sufficient in the wild, you've picked up the right book. My goal is that by the time you finish reading, you will have the expertise and confidence to find delicious and nourishing mushrooms from the bounty of the forest without having to worry about getting poisoned.

If you're new to mushroom hunting and looking for ways to round out your survival skills so that you will be ready and able to live off the land in a time of crisis, this book will give you easy-to-follow instructions so that you can get started foraging for mushrooms right away. Begin that journey without having to worry about taking an accidental trip into outer space (hence the title of this book). With the knowledge you glean from these pages, you will be able to find, identify, and prepare mushrooms with confidence, in a way that doesn't disrupt the natural ecosystem that sustains us all. In fact, you will learn ways to leave the forest a little healthier than you found it.

In my first book, I advised beginning foragers to stay away from mushrooms. Making mistakes while trying to differentiate between edible and poisonous mushrooms can lead to severe illness, hallucinations, and even sudden death. Even if the mushroom you misidentify doesn't kill you instantly, cramps, diarrhea, and disorienting visions are not going to be welcome experiences – particularly in a survival situation. But mushrooms are too valuable a resource to ignore, particularly for those who plan to live off the land for a significant part of their sustenance. There are going to be times and places where game is scarce, and wild greens, although delicious and nutritious, fall short of the calories you're going to need to sustain an active lifestyle out in nature. Wild mushrooms are an excellent source of protein, fiber, antioxidants, and several minerals that are crucial to human survival.

Most of the mushroom guides you'll find catalogue hundreds, if not thousands, of mushrooms. We know of at least 14,000 species, and new varieties are being discovered all the time. The vast majority of these mushrooms are so rare that it's unlikely you'll ever see them. A lot of them are only found in very specific types of environments, like the yartsa gunbu, which only grows in the Himalayas at elevations between 9,000 and 16,000 feet. (And even if you're in the right place, they're still hard to find. They only grow out of the bodies of caterpillars.) Around 3000 species of mushroom are edible but don't worry, you don't need to learn how to ID them all. You will only encounter a fraction of those in your local environment.

In this book, we're going to focus on mushrooms that are:

- Relatively ubiquitous
- Easy to locate and harvest without disrupting the environment
- Palatable (if not downright delicious!)
- Packed with nutrition

We will also take a close look at mushrooms to avoid – both those that are poisonous and those that are edible but look enough like poisonous varieties that it's best to keep hunting until you find a mushroom that's more of a sure bet. You will also learn about the healing powers of medicinal mushrooms and the mysterious properties of the ones that can induce hallucinations and other psychological effects.

In addition to a user-friendly field guide to the most common mushrooms you will see on your foraging expeditions (that's in Chapter 7), we're going to cover a great deal of information that is not only fascinating and useful but could also save your life.

You will read about some of the most awe-inspiring natural environments in the world for hunting mushrooms. I hope you get to explore some of them! Mushrooms, as you will learn, are a whole world unto themselves, and they are an important part of the web of life. Forests depend on them to recycle the nutrients of trees and other plants (and caterpillars in the case of yartsa gunbu). Trees also rely on the mycelial networks of mushrooms, which are something like their root systems, to communicate and share nutrients with each other.

This book will serve as a guide to the most common edible and medicinal mushrooms, as well as some of the fascinating species that are less often encountered. It will provide you with a foundation for understanding the role of fungi in our lives.

By the time you've finished reading this book, you will be well-versed in forest foraging etiquette, and you will understand the laws surrounding mushroom foraging. In addition to learning how to keep yourself safe and fed in the wild, you can be sure that you will be enjoying the bounty of nature without harming the local flora and fauna or risking a run-in with the law.

Learning to forage for mushrooms will connect you to your deepest roots as a human being on this planet. We humans and our mycelial friends have a long and fascinating history together, as foraging for mushrooms is a time-honored activity that goes back through the ages. Mushrooms have been nourishing, healing, and teaching us ever since our first ancestors began their lineage.

I'm excited to see so many new foragers getting interested in learning about mushrooms, and I'm thrilled to have you join us. Let's get started!

CHAPTER ONE

What's so Great About Mushrooms?

I've always loved to hunt for game and forage for wild edible greens on wilderness trips. I can spend weeks backpacking through rugged mountains, completely dependent upon Mother Nature to provide everything I need from day to day. The knowledge that no matter where I go, I can find and prepare something nutritious to eat gives me delicious peace of mind.

For years, I would look at all the different mushrooms I passed by with curiosity, wondering whether they had the power to strike me dead, render me an interplanetary traveler in my mind, or simply add a tasty morsel to my dinner that night. But I never dared. I was under the impression that a highly advanced level of expertise was required before one could pluck a mushroom from the forest with confidence – after all, some varieties in Asia are even poisonous to the touch!

I finally discovered what I had been missing out on all my life on a camping trip in the Ozarks with my friend Doug. He introduced me to the wonders of wild mushrooms by adding a chicken of the woods to my rabbit and purslane stew. (By chicken of the woods I don't mean a wild chicken. It's a type of mushroom.) I watched in admiration and horror as he sliced the spongy yellow meat into my boiling pot.

I was hesitant to eat it at first. I had known this guy since childhood, and we'd been on many hunting trips in the past. I'd never seen him eat a mushroom before. So I had to ask him, "When did you become an expert on mushrooms?"

"I'm not," he grinned. "I don't know much about them at all."

At that point, all I could do was stare. I was hungry, and this rabbit was the only one we'd seen all day. Had Doug just poisoned my dinner?

"But I know *this* mushroom," Doug stated. "There aren't any others like it, so there's no way you could accidentally pick something poisonous instead." He assured me that once you've seen one chicken of the woods, you'll always be able to recognize it.

Hungry enough to take a chance, I dug in. Calling that mushroom chicken of the woods turned out to be a misnomer – it tasted way better than chicken! We shamelessly licked our bowls clean.

That was when it hit me. You don't have to know every last detail about all of the mushrooms in existence before you can start foraging for them. Just like foraging for other wild edibles, you just need to know how to identify the ones you're looking for, get familiar with any look-alikes, and stay away from the unknowns. The skillset does require some dedication, patience, and attention to detail, but it's not rocket science.

Chicken of the woods is a great mushroom for beginners. It actually became my gateway mushroom. The next time I found one I was alone, and I cooked it and ate it with confidence. That same year, I went on to sample pheasant's back mushrooms, shaggy manes, and boletes. I've continued adding more savory forest edibles to my repertoire since then.

Wild mushrooms are a lot of fun to forage, and many of them are as nutritious as they are pleasing to the palate. Mushrooms, particularly the varieties that grow in the wild, are an unsung superfood. They're high in both fiber and protein, and they're low in carbs. Including a good amount of these power snacks in your diet on a regular basis can:

- Reduce your risk of getting cancer
- Help manage metabolic disorders like diabetes
- Keep your heart healthy
- Support a healthy pregnancy
- Increase your white blood cell counts
- Help keep your brain and muscles agile as you age

Mushrooms are packed with a ton of vital nutrients like B vitamins, which are essential for helping your body transform the food you eat into energy, so they're great for regulating your metabolism, controlling your weight, and keeping your energy levels even throughout the day. B vitamins are also mood boosters. They can help you keep your mind clear, and they provide a buffer against stress.

Mushrooms even have the ability to synthesize vitamin D if left in sunlight. Since most mushrooms grow in shaded areas, you will want to allow your mushrooms to bask in sunlight for an hour before you cook and eat them in order to maximize this effect.

Oh, and if you happen to be looking to add riboflavin, niacin, pantothenic acid, phosphorus, or iron to your diet, mushrooms are an excellent source. Morels offer 40 times the recommended amount of iron per calorie. They're also great for Thiamin, Vitamin B6, Potassium, and Zinc, and they provide Vitamin C and Magnesium.

Given how packed with vital nutrients they are, it's not surprising that many mushrooms have medicinal as well as culinary uses. These fungi have an amazing ability to inhibit viruses by binding viral cells. Some mushrooms also increase the body's production of B and T cells, which fight bacterial and viral invaders.

A little-known fact about mushrooms is that they are often used in skin care products. This is because they contain antioxidants that reduce inflammation and phenolic veratric acid, which smooths out wrinkles.

I could go on and on about how good mushrooms are for you. Given all that we know about their health benefits, it amazes me that the average American only eats around three pounds of mushrooms per year. Compare that to the 53 pounds of bread we eat in a year, and it's no wonder there's talk of a national health crisis! In this forager's, humble opinion, foraging for mushrooms and other wild edibles is a great way to reduce your dependence on a food system that is getting increasingly expensive, unreliable, and crowded with foods that only seem to make us sicker, fatter, and more depressed, instead of healthier.

The good news is that more people are becoming interested in mushrooms as they catch onto how nutritious and tasty these little morsels of the forest are. Increasing numbers of people are finding out for themselves how rewarding and fun it can be to go out for a leisurely stroll into the forest, taking in all of nature's mesmerizing details as you collect delicious curiosities just waiting to be found.

Relying on mushrooms for sustenance is nothing new for humanity. Families across all seven continents (well ok, six, not Antarctica) have passed down knowledge about how to harvest and prepare edible mushrooms for generations. While much of our early history with mushrooms has been forgotten, anthropologists have been making some fascinating discoveries about how our forebears have used, revered, and been influenced by them throughout the ages.

CHAPTER TWO
A Brief (But Epic) History of Humans and Mushrooms

It's not uncommon for bonobos, our closest relatives in the Animal Kingdom, to graze on mushrooms. Something like sixty other primate species include them in their diets as well. So, it's probably safe to say that humans have been consuming mushrooms (with varying results) for thousands of years.

Given that some mushrooms have interesting effects on our brains, there is some scientific curiosity about whether mushrooms, specifically those containing psychoactive compounds like psilocybin, a chemical compound that causes hallucinations and other effects on the human brain, could have influenced human evolution. This idea is known as the "stoned ape theory." According to some neuroscientists, the chemicals in mushrooms that our early ancestors ate could have switched certain genes on or off and rewired their brains at a genetic level, making us as a species more imaginative, adventurous, cooperative, and communicative.

Anthropologists postulate that the first time a hominid had the opportunity to eat a magic mushroom could have been about two million years ago, which is right around the time humans went through rapid evolutionary changes and our brains tripled in size. Coincidence? I have no idea. Some say it isn't, but we'll probably never know for sure.

What we do know is that humans have benefited from ordinary non-psychoactive mushrooms in their everyday lives, beginning long before we began documenting our coexistence with mushrooms in our written histories. Our ancestors cooked with them, used them to treat illnesses and injuries, and even used them to carry the embers of their campfires on long treks through damp forests at a time when lighters hadn't been invented yet.

Much of our ancient knowledge about mushrooms has inevitably been lost, but we are starting to recover it as scientists make exciting discoveries about our past.

Mushrooms as Medicine

A great example of this is the discovery of the remains of Otzi, the mummified "iceman" found high in the Alps back in 1991. Over five thousand years ago, Otzi was shot in the back with an arrow while making the dangerous trek through the mountains. This would have been quite an endeavor, even for a man in the prime of his health. Otzi was suffering from intestinal parasites that caused acute pain, and his right hand was badly injured. This pre-historic CSI episode rendered fascinating conclusions.

Medicinal tea made from birch polypore, the type of mushroom Otzi carried, has been found to be remarkably potent for treating exactly the type of parasites he had. The mushroom can also be used to clean wounds, reduce inflammation, and control bleeding – all useful applications for his wounded hand. These realizations inspired a series of clinical studies that uncovered further medicinal properties of this mushroom, which is common wherever you see birch trees. Since the discovery of Otzi's ancient med kit in 1991, birch polypore has been used in experimental cancer treatments, and its role as an important natural remedy for a variety of ailments and injuries has been revived. (See Chapter Seven for more on this amazing mushroom.)

Foraging as a Way of Life

Wild mushrooms were an important food staple as well as a source of medicine in pre-agricultural societies, where much of what people ate was foraged and hunted. And even after people began cultivating crops and raising livestock in agrarian villages, they continued to pass down ancestral knowledge of which mushrooms were safe to eat so that they could fall back on the provisions of the forest during bad years when harvests were unreliable.

People in Eastern Europe, Slavic countries in particular, have maintained mushroom hunting as an important part of their culture, and this is reflected in their cuisine. Flip through any traditional Polish cookbook, and you will find stews, dumplings, fermented and pickled dishes. One of the nation's favorite traditional Christmas recipes in Poland is a delicious wild mushroom soup.

Mushroom foraging in Poland is almost considered a basic human right – something everyone should learn to do and something that should never be restricted. You can pick mushrooms just about anywhere on public lands in Poland, no permits required.

Until very recently, there was a sharp divide between mushroom-loving cultures in the East and mushroom-fearing cultures in the West. Mushroom hunting carried on in Eastern European countries like Poland, Russia, and Bulgaria, while it was almost completely forgotten in the West for centuries.

There are a few explanations for this. When Christianity spread across Europe and pagan religions that involved psychoactive mushrooms died out, edible mushrooms were demonized along with the varieties that were associated with religious rituals and spiritual experiences. Human nature has never been good at discernment, and so, since certain mushrooms were used in pagan rituals, and others were actually deadly, all mushrooms developed a cultural association with danger. Even the most harmless and delicious species were called names like witches' butter, devil's fingers, and Satan's bolete.

Pastures and meadows where mushrooms naturally grow in circles were considered cursed and unlucky. People kept their cows from grazing near these "fairy rings" because they believed it would curdle the milk. At least 50 species of mushrooms grow in this pattern, some of which are highly sought after and some of which are toxic.

Another reason mushrooms were feared was because they had a reputation for transforming Viking warriors into Berserkers; fearless and bloodthirsty killers who were somehow invincible to their enemies' weapons. It is likely true that the Berserkers consumed liberty caps, another species of psychoactive mushrooms, before going into battle, but they didn't make the Vikings bloodthirsty or invincible. The real-life effects of liberty caps are said to be very similar to LSD with visual distortions and hallucinations.

No doubt, there were still at least a few furtive foragers among the peasant classes, but the art of mushroom hunting was almost entirely forgotten in the British Isles, Germany, Spain, and France. Why risk getting burned at the stake? In Eastern Europe, where harvesting mushrooms was not stigmatized, foraging for mushrooms is still a popular holiday activity for families and people of all ages.

French haute cuisine reintroduced mushrooms to the western palate in the nineteenth century, and suddenly they were featured on hors d'oeuvres tables in all of society's finest homes and restaurants. The bestselling cookbook that ushered in the twentieth century was titled *One Hundred Mushroom Receipts*, by Kate Sargeant. Mushrooms have been steadily increasing in popularity since then.

Ancient and Modern Psychedelic Culture

Something like 200 species of mushrooms containing psilocybin are sprinkled across the globe, and people seeking novel and/or spiritual experiences have been consuming them since the beginning of time. Psychoactive mushrooms may or may not have contributed to the physiology of our brains, but without a doubt, they had an impact on early human cultures.

A cave painting in Spain that dates back to 9,000 years ago depicts a line of masked dancers each holding a mushroom in their right hand, with lines drawn connecting the mushrooms to their heads. A nearby image shows, according to ethnobotanist Terrence McKenna (1993), "shamans [who are] dancing with fists full of mushrooms and also have mushrooms sprouting out of their bodies. In one instance they are shown running joyfully, surrounded by the geometric structures of their hallucinations." One of these mushroom shamans, drawn with the body of a bee for his head, has become an icon of contemporary psychedelic culture.

The Mycelial Roots of Halloween

Regardless of what our ancestors were trying to accomplish with these mushrooms and rituals, we do have concrete evidence of the influence that more recent use of psilocybin has had on traditions that we hold and stories we tell to this day. I'm talking specifically about our Halloween traditions, which came from the ancient druids and poets of Ireland.

Poets in ancient Ireland held an influential if not outright politically powerful position in society. They were believed to possess *imbas forosnai*, which means the gift of clairvoyant inspiration in Old Irish. They received this inspiration after chewing on the red flesh of the fly-agaric, a psilocybin mushroom, and lying in a dark room. When they emerged, they told tales of the leprechauns, fairies, and other mystical beings that became the basis of pagan religious beliefs throughout Ireland. To this day, when people in Ireland talk about going "off with the faeries" or "away with the pixies" it's generally understood that they're talking about going on a mushroom trip. The Gaelic word *pookies* means both faeries and mushrooms.

Ancient religious leaders in Siberia and Scandinavia are believed to have eaten fly-agarics as well, and the indigenous religions of these areas also feature magical beings that live in the forests and are only visible at particular times.

Fly-agaric mushrooms are also known as toadstools. Even if you don't recognize the name and have never seen them in the wild, I guarantee you've seen pictures of them. These are the mushrooms with the shiny red caps and white spots that are featured in folkloric art and cartoons, often with pixies, leprechauns, and faeries dancing on them, sitting around them having tea parties, or using them for umbrellas.

If you're my age or older, you're probably thinking about the Smurfs right now. This was a Saturday morning cartoon about a village of little blue people with white caps who lived in toadstools and fled in terror every time a malicious wizard came around trying to capture and eat them. What you may not know is that the Smurfs were the creation of a Belgian cartoonist in the 1950s, so they weren't a direct product of Irish folklore. They are an example of the way mythical little people have come to be associated with toadstools across cultures.

Late October is when fly agarics pop out of the forest floor, just in time for Halloween and other harvest season festivities. This was the time of year that the ancient Celts believed the veil that separated the living from the dead grew thin. The living could more easily enter other realms, and the spirits of those who had passed away could walk the earth again. It's likely that what made these beliefs plausible were hallucinations brought on by eating fly-agarics.

I imagine that the visions of the walking dead people experienced around Halloween probably had something to do with the general state of mind in agrarian societies at that time of year. This was a time for celebration if you had enjoyed a good growing season and gotten all of your harvest in on time. If the rains were late or the frost was early and if you hadn't accumulated enough supplies to keep you and your family alive through the long dark winter, this was a time of fear and dread.

Even if you've never partaken of psychoactive mushrooms, the society you live in wouldn't be what it is today without their influence on past generations. They've given our culture its collective fascination with enchantment, mystical worlds, and magic.

Magic Mushrooms in the New World

Hallucinogenic mushrooms have a long history in the Americas as well as in Europe. While the Christianized inhabitants of Western Europe left their ritual use of psychedelic mushrooms in the long-forgotten past, the descendants of the ancient Mayan and Aztecs kept their traditions alive in secret, practicing hidden ceremonies in humble villages across Central and South America.

An American mushroom researcher visiting a small village in Oaxaca, Mexico was the first outsider to witness a religious ceremony in which psychedelic mushrooms were consumed. It was 1955. Two years later, he published an article in Life magazine, the nation's leading news publication at the time, called "Seeking the Magic Mushroom." Over the next decade or so, thousands of counter-culture enthusiasts found their way to that village and experienced the magical effects he had described first-hand, thanks to the only shaman who would accommodate them, Maria Sabina.

Maria Sabina's community members quickly got fed up with the outsiders who didn't show respect for their rituals and behaved badly while they were under the influence of psilocybin. Angry with her for profiting off their culture's sacred knowledge while bringing dangerous exposure and general mayhem to their village, they burned her house down and had her arrested. Best not to offend the sensibilities of an entire culture when living among them.

Magic mushrooms were legal in the United States for a little over a decade before the revelers and mystical seekers who ate them captured the attention of the authorities. They were banned in 1969, and other countries in Europe and the Americas soon followed suit.

The relationships that humans have carried on with mushrooms certainly have varied throughout the ages and around the world. As we increase our scientific knowledge and technological acumen, we humans are turning another corner in our relationship with the world of mushrooms. Each year we discover exciting new ways they can help us live in closer harmony with God's grand design.

CHAPTER THREE

Who Loves Mushrooms, Aside from You and Me?

Mushrooms are so much more than tasty treats, medicine, and providers of mystical experiences. They may hold the key to some of the food security issues that are on the horizon. Given their nutritional value, my belief is that if they had a more prominent place in our diets, we would be a healthier more nourished people. Mushrooms are natural protectors of the ecosystems in most places where they are found, providing a buffer against changing environmental conditions. Researchers are finding new applications for them in micro-forestry, and they're even used to aid in search and rescue operations.

Mushrooms for the Future

Here in the United States, we have a culture that ethnobotanists refer to as "mycophobic." In plain English, most of us have been conditioned to fear wild mushrooms. As a culture, I would say that we fear wild edibles in general. Most of us were not raised by parents or grandparents who regularly took us into natural places and taught us how to identify various types of edible plants and mushrooms. If you try offering food that has not been packaged, labeled with an expiration date, and purchased at a grocery store to your average American, they probably wouldn't dare take a bite.

Case in point: I sometimes take small groups on tours of my some of my forager farms (see Chapter Six of my book *Master of Edible Wild Plants* for info on how to set up your own for free). On the tour, I point out all the wild edible plants that I consume as part of my everyday diet. I then offer salads, veggie platters, soups, and other snacks made from my freshly harvested produce. My visitors are rarely adventurous enough to sample much beyond the carrots and kale chips. At the end of the tour, one woman looked out at my garden, a riotous half acre of greens, colorful flowers, and blossoming fruit trees and said, "So the only plants you have that you're really supposed to eat are carrots, cabbage and onions?" Supposed to eat? What a sheltered existence we live.

Other cultures, particularly in Eastern Europe where the Slavic and Romantic languages are spoken, are a completely different story. As I mentioned in Chapter Two, it's common for people in these cultures to grow up learning to forage, cook with, and feast on a variety of mushrooms. Anywhere people are consuming mushroom-based dishes on a daily basis, they are benefiting from the vital nutrients they provide. They're also getting plenty of dietary fiber, something that is lacking in a lot of American diets, and they are able to consume ample protein without having to depend on industrially produced meat (don't get me started on that!).

Not to be a downer, but food insecurity is a man created problem that the various governments of the world seem to be determined to make worse. You need only look to the protesting Dutch farmers of Europe to see that authority figures of every stripe are either unwilling or unable to understand the importance of food supply chains. The standard processed meat and grain diet that Americans and other Westerners have adopted for generations is unhealthy and getting harder to sustain. Industrial food production is getting more expensive as healthy soil is abused by monocropping and water system mismanagement creates unnecessary crises.

Fortunately, many in the West are wising up and getting back to our roots when it comes to wild foods. As a culture, we have been gradually losing the fear of mushrooms that gripped us for over two centuries. The mushrooms we can buy in grocery stores and have served in restaurants today are not the shocking sight they would have been to Americans and Western Europeans a century ago.

I am encouraged to see so many people are getting serious about learning healthy and sustainable ways to feed themselves. My hope is that we are freely transitioning to a culture of mycophiles (instead of mycophobes) and lovers of all the nutritious bounty that nature freely provides. On the other side of that transition, we're bound to become a much healthier society, since at least six percent of edible mushrooms are known to help prevent some of the most common health-related diseases that plague us today.

Fungi Actively Protect and Restore the Environment

Some of the most encouraging updates I've seen from the world of science have had to do with… you guessed it! Mushrooms. Fungi are now being used to clean up oil spills and other toxic sites, recycle plastic, and produce eco-friendly fabrics and building materials. The byproducts of most of these processes are wholesome nutrition, so win, win! Let's take a quick look at a few of the ways mushrooms are helping us keep the planet healthy for future generations.

Plastic pollution is everywhere. 150 million tons of plastic has found its way to the oceans, where it floats and drifts in what are known as great garbage patches. We didn't think anything in the natural world was equipped to deal with the mess until student researchers discovered that several common species of fungi can eat it. They break down and absorb every molecule, cleaning it up without a trace! Some species can even do this in completely dark and anaerobic conditions, like the bottom of landfills where a lot of plastics and other materials that don't easily decompose end up.

In the last ten years, we've found fifty types of fungi that breakdown plastic, including one popular delicacy of the forest – oyster mushrooms. An Austrian lab has prototyped a small oyster mushroom farm that lives on post-consumer plastic. The mushrooms this farm produces are reportedly every bit as delicious as the specimens you'll find in the grocery store. I don't think there's any way it could compete with wild oysters from the forest, but it still looks like progress to me!

That's not all that mushrooms are doing for the planet. They have also been put to work breaking down other petroleum-based products besides plastics and pharmaceuticals that would otherwise take centuries to return to the earth. Instead of being left to slowly release toxins into the environment, these would-be pollutants are efficiently converted into fungi, sometimes even producing edible mushrooms.

And there's more. Some species of mushrooms eat phosphorus, which causes them to glow in the dark. These fungi are being put to work in hazardous areas that are contaminated with leftover ammunition and landmines that are hard to locate. When the fungi consume the phosphorus and sprout bioluminescent mushrooms, hazmat cleanup crews can see what needs to be done where. Not exactly the rapid minesweeping we relied on in Afghanistan, but effective, nonetheless.

It's amazing enough that fungi can eat plastic. It turns out that they can be used to create plastic-like materials too. Producing conventional plastics requires enormous amounts of energy and emits toxic pollutants into the air we breathe. Even if all the plastic we produce and throw away were fed to mushrooms, we can't go on producing it forever.

Mycelia are now beginning to replace foam packing materials (peanuts etc.) made from polystyrene. Something like 90% of polystyrene products currently end up in landfills instead of being recycled, where they will take thousands of years to break down. These plastics break down into smaller and smaller particles instead of decomposing the way organic material does, and so they stay with us. Microscopic particles have been found in the bloodstreams of people and animals all over the world.

Mushroom-based packing materials, on the other hand, can be tossed into your garden when you're done with them, and all they will do is improve the soil. The way they are produced is much more environmentally friendly as well. Instead of being injected into molds, they grow into them while feeding on agricultural byproducts like seed husks and straw.

Mushrooms (and the fungi that produce them) are an integral part of the natural world. In fact, they often make the difference between a thriving forest and a struggling one. One of the most important jobs fungi do is breaking down dead organic matter into nutrients that plants can assimilate. Without mushrooms, forests would eventually be reduced to piles of dead plant matter decomposing at an excruciatingly slow pace.

Fungi complete the cycle of life by recycling nutrients from dying and decaying plants and making them available to new seedlings and sprouts. Remember that fungi are similar to animals in that they can digest organic matter and break it down into minerals that plants can use. Plants can't do that for themselves.

Many common tree species including maple, western red cedar, and Douglas fir would not survive at all without fungi to break down and transport nutrients for them. The way mushrooms help them is by building underground networks of mycelia that connect the surrounding plants and trees to each other. Trees use these networks to communicate and share nutrients.

Bacteria use these networks as well. They can travel incredible distances on what mycologists (scientists who devote their studies to the world of mushrooms) sometimes refer to as the living world's natural internet.

Mushrooms and the Climate

Fungi are incredibly responsive to changes in their environments. They almost seem to be making calculated and intelligent decisions at times. Scientists have realized that the decisions fungi make need to be factored into calculations about how the natural world changes. It turns out that fungi have an impact on climate by releasing and sequestering carbon. When fungi experience environmental stresses, changes in the climate for example, they respond by bulking up their mycelia and strengthening their cell wall, which means sequestering more carbon. At the same time, they shift their focus away from decomposing organic matter, which means they're releasing less carbon into the atmosphere.

The impact mushrooms can have on the climate is difficult to imagine when you think of how small most mushrooms are, but keep in mind that the capped little morsels we find poking out of the forest litter and spreading along decomposing logs are only a small part of the whole organism. The bulk of a given fungus is usually found in its mycelia. True, these root-like threads are usually no thicker than a strand of hair, but they make up for their delicate build by spreading for miles underground, forming intricate networks that can connect thousands of trees.

The largest known organism in the world is a single fungus, thousands of years old, that covers three and a half square miles underneath the surface of the Blue Mountains in the Malheur National Forest in Oregon. This Fungus Humongous (not its actual scientific name) weighs an estimated 400 tons. With that much biomass, it has the capacity to sequester huge amounts of carbon underground.

This particular specimen plays a role that is somewhat complicated. Some fungi carry on mutually beneficial relationships with the plants that host them while others engage in more parasitic relationships. The largest mushroom in the world is of the latter variety. *Armillaria ostoyae* grow by extending shoelace-like mycelia along the roots of conifer trees, spreading a lethal root disease from tree to tree along with the digestive enzymes it excretes. It also produces truckloads of sweet mushrooms that pair well with garlic and herbs and taste amazing when roasted or added to soups.

Note: Be extremely cautious if you ever decide to harvest honey mushrooms. There is at least one deadly look-alike.

Members of the Armillaria genus and other parasitic fungi don't usually kill healthy trees. More often, they hasten the death of trees that are already old and sick. They continue to digest a tree's dense cellulose long after the trunk has fallen. These are the grim reapers of the forest community. Without their assistance, dead trees would take centuries to decompose and make their nutrients available to the next generation of forest plants. (With the help of these fungi, the process usually only takes decades.)

Parasitic fungi paired with the right kinds of plants can actually make a forest healthier, particularly the ones that feed on the bacteria that make trees and other plants sick. When parasitic fungi are part of a balanced ecosystem, they typically only feed on trees that are already weakened or sick.

But sometimes, as is the case with our ancient underground behemoth in Oregon, a parasitic fungus can wreak havoc in a forest where it doesn't belong. Some two thousand years ago, when the fungus was just starting out, the above-ground forest that hosted it likely looked very different from what it looks like today, and the fungus probably had a more positive relationship with the types of trees that it grew up with. The Douglas fir trees that dominate the forest now are being attacked and killed in their prime.

Now that you know about the many ways humans and non-humans have benefited from mushrooms, I'll bet you're getting curious about what makes them tick. Did you know that they're not plants? And they're not animals either. What are they, you ask? You'll find out in Chapter Four!

CHAPTER FOUR
What is a Mushroom, Anyway?

As with any kind of treasure hunt, before you go looking for mushrooms it helps to develop a good understanding of what exactly it is that you're looking for. Knowing at the very least how mushrooms feed and reproduce will give you some excellent clues as to when and where to find them.

In these next few chapters, we will talk about what mushrooms are, how they live, who their friends are, and how to get along with them. It sounds like I'm talking more about animals or people than a kind of plant, doesn't it?

Well, it turns out that mushrooms aren't plants, exactly, but they're not members of the animal kingdom either. So, what are they?

The Feeding Habits of Mushrooms

Plants, by definition, get their energy through photosynthesis. They can directly utilize nutrients in the soil to fulfill all of their sustenance needs. Animals, including human animals, can't do that. For the majority of our caloric and nutritional needs, we produce enzymes to break down other organisms (plants and animals) so we can digest their nutrients.

Mushrooms do that too. So when you look at the way organisms feed, you could say that mushrooms are more similar to people than they are to plants. I don't know about you, but I think that's pretty wild. There's even a taxonomic word for organisms that feed the way we do. You, me, your dog, birds and fish, and mushrooms in the forest – we are all heterotrophs.

The main difference between the way we members of the Animal Kingdom get sustenance and the way mushrooms do it is that they don't use internal digestive systems. Instead of bringing food inside their bodies to digest it, they secrete enzymes externally, digest the food, and then absorb it.

I should say that fungi digest their food this way, not mushrooms. The mushrooms themselves are not the entire organism, they're just the fruiting body (we can't simply call them fruit because they don't grow on plants) of fungi. The purpose of the mushroom is mainly to produce spores for reproduction, while digestion takes place underground in the mushroom's root-like structure, a delicate web of threads called mycelia.

Knowing how fungi feed and what they feed on will give you important clues if you want to know where to find the most delicious wild mushrooms, since most mushrooms grow on or near the surfaces of the organisms that give them sustenance. Each species of fungi has its own nutritional needs and relies on different types of host organisms. Some form mutually beneficial relationships with the trees that host them while others are parasitic. Many types of fungus prefer host organisms that are decaying or already dead. These fungi help return nutrients to the forest floor, making them available to future generations of seedlings.

Trees are an almost universal favorite food source among mushrooms because they provide moisture and temperature regulation in addition to nutrients. Some types of mushrooms only grow at the base of living trees, some grow out of the bark on the trunks, and some only grow out of decaying logs on the ground. This is why a mushroom's location in proximity to trees or other types of plants is often such an important part of mushroom identification.

There are about fifty species of mushroom-producing fungi that feed on decomposing organic matter that is distributed throughout the soil in meadows and glades. Over time, their mycelia grow into a dense underground mat that forms in a circle under the turf. When it's time to reproduce, the organisms send mushrooms up at their outer perimeters, forming what we like to call a fairy ring.

Four Types of Fungi that Produce Mushrooms

There are four basic types of fungi: mycorrhizal, saprotrophic, endophytic, and parasitic. I know what you're probably wondering right now, and the answer is no. These four categories won't tell you which are poisonous, which are good to eat, which are medicinal, and which will send you to distant planets. These categories group fungi by how they function in the ecosystems in which they are found.

Mycorrhizal Fungi

Mycorrhizal fungi grow their mycelia around the roots of the trees that host them. Their relationship with these trees is mutually beneficial. The fungi receive sugar that trees produce via photosynthesis, and the trees receive water and nutrients from the mycelia that cover their roots. The mycelia also filter toxins out of the water that they deliver to their host trees, and some of them excrete enzymes that protect certain species of trees from diseases. Most trees with mycorrhizal friends entwined in their roots are more tolerant of stress, less susceptible to frost, and grow faster than trees that don't have fungal friends.

Most species of mycorrhizal fungus evolved to share their life with specific tree species. Some are only found in deciduous forests while others only grow with conifers. Chanterelles are found under hardwoods like birch, maple, oak, and poplar.

These fungi are not territorial, so you will often find multiple species of mushrooms under a single tree. Not all of them are edible either though, so you will always want to be aware of any toxic look-alikes mingling with the specimens you are seeking.

Saprotrophic Fungi

Saprotrophic fungi are the clean-up crew of the forest. They help plants complete their lifecycle by decomposing dead organic material and transforming it into nutrients that plants can use. Some saprotrophic fungi begin working on a host plant before it has actually died, but none require a living host. Many common edible mushrooms including cremini, shiitake, portabella, and morels are saprotrophic.

Some, like morels, break down litter on the forest floor. They can often be found where papery old leaves and rotting twigs are particularly deep. The types that break down decaying wood produce mushrooms that can be found on logs and on the trunks of trees that are nearing the end of their lives.

Parasitic Fungi

Fungi that are parasitic attach themselves to healthy organisms and weaken them. Some harm their hosts by introducing diseases, others slowly take over by coopting their host's tissues from the inside out. While all the fungi in the other three categories of mushroom-producers limit themselves to hosts in the plant kingdom, parasitic mushrooms can sometimes be found growing out of the bodies of insects.

Parasitic fungi aren't usually good news for the forests, but they do have some redeeming qualities. Many of the medicines derived from mushrooms are produced by members of this category.

Endophytic Fungi

I want to briefly mention a fourth category of fungi that doesn't really belong in this book because it doesn't produce mushrooms. Endophytic fungi live their entire lives within the bodies of host organisms (plants and animals). They are often microscopic, sometimes parasitic. Plants that host endophytes rarely show symptoms of infection, and some of these fungi are even beneficial. They do produce spores that are transported by the wind or carried by insects, but they do this without forming a fruiting body, so they're of no real concern to our purposes.

Mushroom Reproduction

One way that mushrooms differ from both plants and animals is the way they reproduce. As I mentioned above, mushrooms are the fruiting body of fungi, and their purpose is primarily reproductive. But they don't produce seeds the way the fruits of plants do. Instead, they produce millions of tiny spores that float on the breeze like dust float on water, or they simply scatter on the forest floor. Mushroom spores can fuse with the spores of other mushrooms to create new life, but they don't have to. Mushroom reproduction is asexual most of the time.

When a spore (or fused pair of spores) finds a suitable location, it germinates and begins to develop rudimentary tubes that grow into complex mycelial structures. Mushrooms are produced when the mycelium is fully mature. How long all of this takes depends on the availability of nutrients, ambient temperature, moisture, and other environmental conditions. Under ideal conditions, this process can often be completed in a matter of days or weeks. However, in most locations where wild mushrooms grow the conditions are only ideal once or twice per year, and so mushroom hunting tends to be very seasonal.

Now that you know what exactly mushrooms are, how they live, and what kinds of environments they thrive in, you're much more likely to spot more of them next time you're in the forest. But will you be able to tell whether the mushrooms you see are safe to eat?

In order to tell the edible mushrooms in your local forest apart from poisonous look-alikes, you're going to need to learn something about mushroom anatomy. No, they don't have legs or arms. Most do have gills, but they're not like the gills of a fish. By the time you're done reading Chapter 5, you will be aware of all the different forms mushrooms can take, and you will be able to classify mushrooms into basic categories, which will help you more accurately pinpoint exactly which species they are and avoid any fatal mistakes.

CHAPTER FIVE
Mushroom Anatomy

As I mentioned in Chapter Three, a fungus at Malheur National Forest in Oregon is believed to be the largest organism in the world. This discovery was reported widely in headlines that said the world's largest lifeform was a mushroom. The headlines were quickly followed by photoshopped images of enormous mushrooms standing among mossy tree trunks, and of course those images went viral on the internet. Park rangers reported that people from all over the country flocked to Malheur hoping to get a glimpse of this gigantic specimen.

Fact checkers at Wafflesatnoon.com traced the photos back to the lab of Tom Bruns, a Professor of Fungal Ecology at Berkely. Bruns readily admitted that the photos were a prank. He identified them as *boletus photoshopus*, "pictured in its natural habitat, the digital photo."

It's true that the fungus in question, an *Armillaria ostoyae*, is as big as 200 gray whales. But that's the whole fungus, not the mushroom. The honey mushrooms that this fungus produces stand anywhere from two to six inches tall.

This is why, throughout this book, I've made an effort to say mushrooms when I'm talking about mushrooms, the fruiting body of fungi, and fungi when I'm talking about the whole enchilada, mycelia and all.

We've established that a mushroom is just one part of a fungus, not the whole thing. What other parts do fungi have? We'll cover that, plus the parts of mushrooms that you will need to know for proper identification so that you can forage with confidence.

The main parts of a mushroom-producing fungus are the sporophore (that's the scientific word for the fruiting body, or mushroom in everyday parlance) and the mycelium, which usually grows underground.

From species to species, there's a lot of variety among mushrooms. Most (but not all) of them sport the familiar stem-and-cap configuration, but they come in other shapes and configurations as well. Most have gills, some have pores, teeth, or ridges instead. Most capped mushrooms are at least partially covered by a veil while they're still immature, and there's a lot of variety in veil structures too.

You learned in Chapter Three that there are four scientific classifications of fungi based on the roles they play in the forests in which they are found. Another way to classify mushrooms is by their anatomical features and the way they look. People have various ways of grouping mushrooms. The categories that I find useful are:

- Gilled mushrooms
- Bolete Types
- Spine fungi
- Coral/fan-like fungi
- Polypores and crust-fungi
- Puffballs and earthstars
- Jellies
- Morels and morel-like mushrooms
- Cup fungi
- Truffles and truffle-like mushrooms
- A few other non-conformists

Agaric (Gilled) Mushrooms

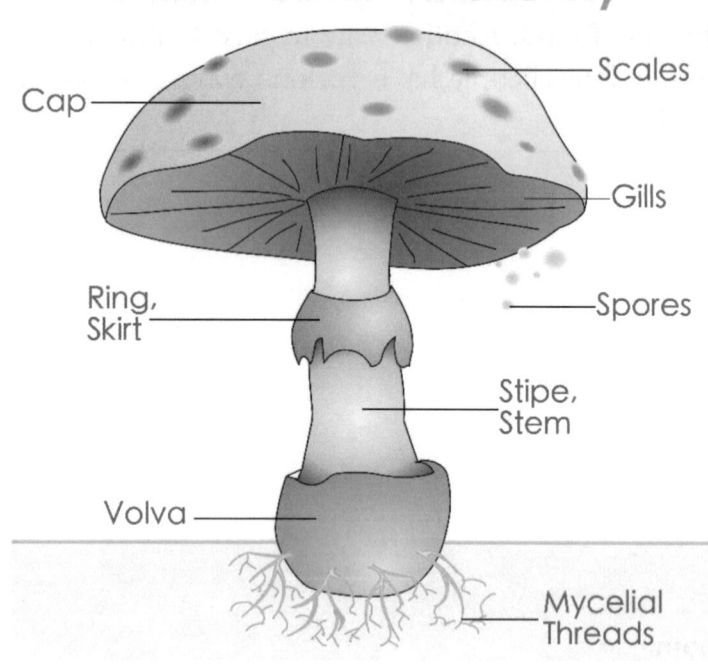

Gilled mushrooms look like what you would think of as a traditional mushroom. The majority of the mushrooms you will ever see fit into this category. They have rounded caps and proportionate stems (on mushrooms they're called stipes). When you pick them and turn them upside down, you can see that the color and texture of the underside of the cap is very different from the top. You will find gill-like ridges or plates that radiate out from the center of the stipe.

The gills of these mushrooms and the spores they produce come in a whole spectrum of colors. With some species, if you blot the gills on a piece of paper and let it sit overnight, the resulting spore print will help you identify the mushroom.

Other keys to identifying gilled mushrooms include:

- Whether the gills merge together close to the stipe or remain separate
- Whether the gills are connected to the stipe, run down the stipe, or whether there's a gap between the gills and the stipe
- Whether each gill runs the length of the cap's radius or whether they merge together and separate at various points.

In addition to the stipe, cap, and gills, most agaric mushrooms start out with a thin veil that covers and protects the developing spores. Some veils cover just the cap and part of the stem. Mushrooms that grow out of the ground often have a veil that covers the entire mushroom. The veil will usually be gone by the time you find and harvest your mushroom, but it often leaves important clues that will help you determine what kind of mushroom you've got.

Identifying Species of Agaric Mushrooms

Once you've determined that the mushroom you're dealing with is of the agaric variety, you will want to figure out exactly what kind of agaric mushroom you have found.

You will be looking at the cap and stipe for shape, color, texture, and size.

Caps can be smooth or scaly, or they can have a rough surface. The shape of the cap varies from species to species. It also changes throughout a mushroom's lifecycle, so you can often tell how old a mushroom is by the shape of the cap.

You will want to get familiar with the following cap shapes:

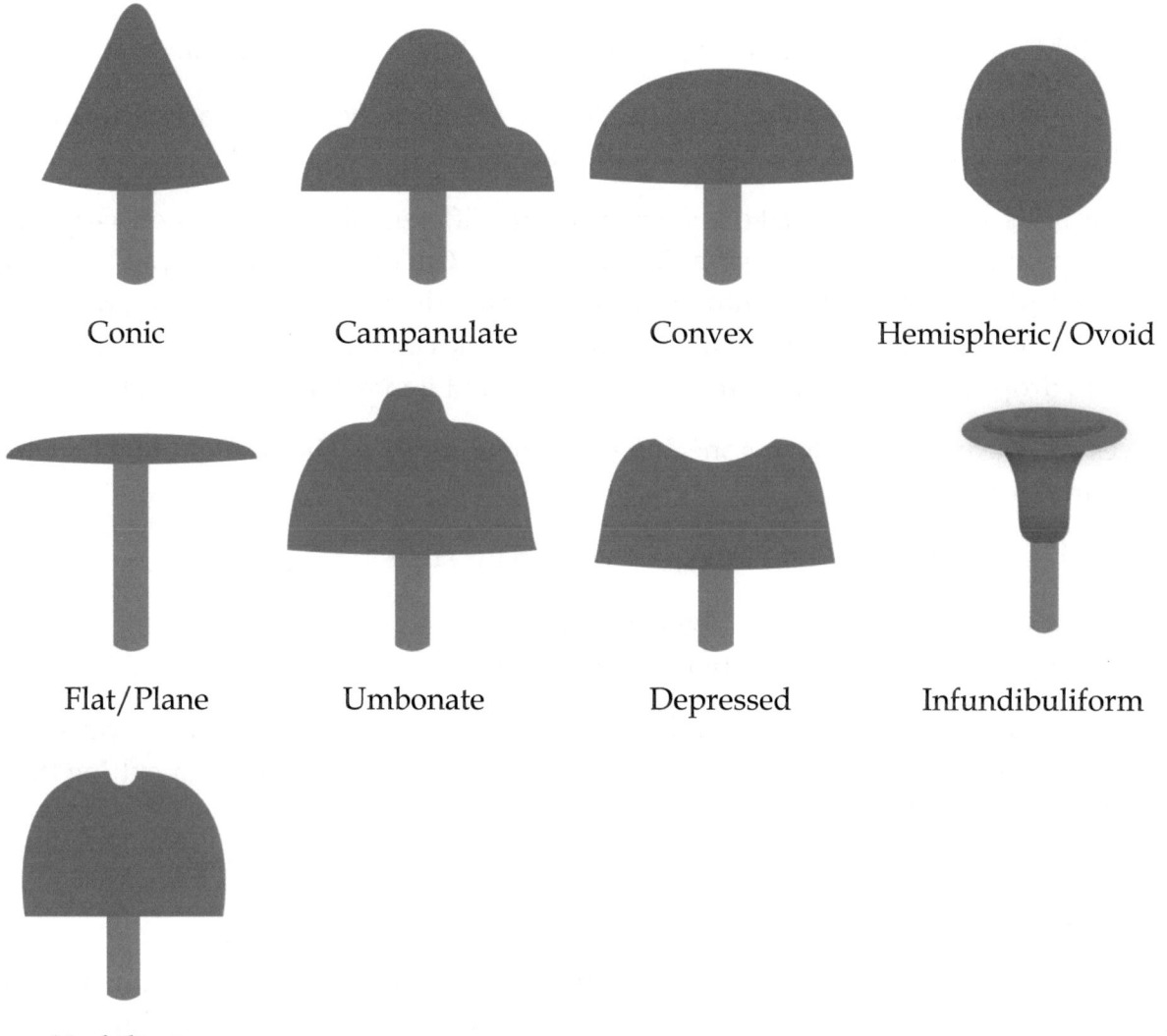

Conic   Campanulate   Convex   Hemispheric/Ovoid

Flat/Plane   Umbonate   Depressed   Infundibuliform

Umbilicate

Stipes can be attached directly to the middle of the cap's underside, or they can be off-center. Their surfaces are covered in fine dots, scab-like patches, or a network of fine grooves. Their shapes are usually as follows:

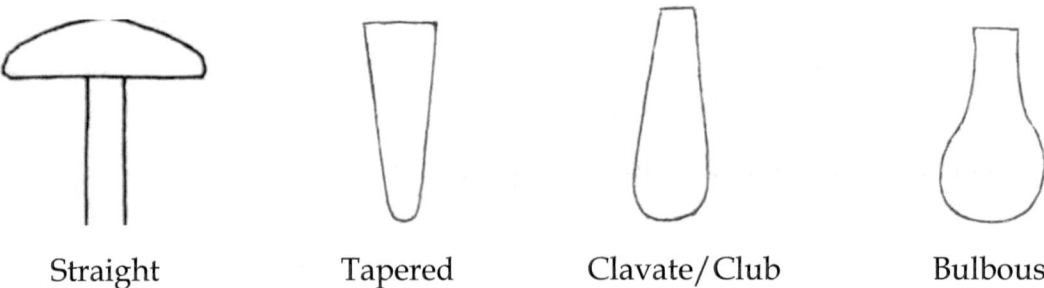

Straight Tapered Clavate/Club Bulbous

Next, you will want to examine the gills. Notice whether they are attached to the stipe, whether they are notched, and how crowded they are.

Sometimes it's necessary to make a spore print to differentiate between two very similar mushroom species. The process is very quick and simple. Cut off the stem and put the cap on a white piece of paper or a piece of aluminum foil, gill-side down. If the cap is dry, drop a little water on top to encourage it to release its spores. Cover the cap with a glass or cup and wait for the spores to drop. You can check it after twelve hours, but it may take up to twenty-four.

Chances are, the veil will be long gone, but you can usually see tell-tale signs of what kind of veil a mushroom had.

- Partial veils will often leave a ring part-way up the stipe.

- Some mushrooms are characterized by little white spots that remain sticking to the surface of the cap after the rest of the veil is gone.

- Mushrooms that are covered entirely with a veil have a volva; a ring all the way down at the base. You may need to dig up some mushrooms instead of picking or cutting them in order to see whether they have a volva.

Bolete Types

There is a genus of fungi called boletes, and there is an edible mushroom commonly called the king bolete. There are other mushrooms that look like boletes but aren't related. For our purposes, I'm grouping them all as bolete types. Like gilled mushrooms, they usually have a well-defined cap and stipe, although the stipe tends to be thicker and rounder.

Instead of gills under the cap, you will find a layer of spongy porous tissue that easily separates from the underside of the caps. This feature is pretty distinctive, but if you're still not sure whether you're dealing with a bolete, just leave it out on the kitchen counter overnight. At room temperature, boletes will turn into an odiferous mass of slimy goo, frequently inhabited by the writhing larvae of tiny flies. Don't let that put you off, though. Most boletes are good to eat as long as you prepare them immediately or keep them refrigerated.

Warning: do not eat bolete-types that have red pores, turn blue when bruised, or produce blue spore prints. Not all boletes are edible so be sure you know which kind you're dealing with.

Identifying Bolete-Type Mushrooms

Pay attention to the species of trees growing in the vicinity of your boletes. Also note the color and texture of the caps, the color of the pores, and the shape, color, and texture of the stipe. Some boletes can be identified by the way they bruise when they are squeezed or cut open.

Spine Mushrooms

At first glance, the many varieties of hedgehog mushrooms can look a lot like gilled mushrooms, but when you peek under the caps you will see tooth-like structures that hang down like icicles. These are a variety of spine fungi.

The spines, sometimes called teeth, can be fine and relatively smooth, or they can be long and shaggy. Some spine fungi have a cap but no stipe, and some have a stipe but no cap. One known family of spine mushrooms, Hericium, doesn't have a cap or a stipe. It puts out its spines on small branch-like structures. Most spine mushrooms are easy to identify because they are so distinctive.

Other Stipe-and-Cap Mushrooms

This category includes mushrooms that have a cap or cap-like structure that sits on top of a stipe, but other than that, they look nothing like what you might consider a garden-variety mushroom. They don't have the typical rounded caps with gills, teeth, or spongey undersides. Morels, with their wrinkled walnut-like heads, belong to this category. Some are shaped like cups, bowls, or saddles. Their stipes can be thick or wire-thin, very short, wrinkled, and sometimes hollow.

Cup Mushrooms

These mushrooms have what could be considered inside-out caps that curl up and inward from the edges. They produce spores inside the cups and eject them forcibly into the air. Most cups are hard to find because they are so small. The edible varieties don't have a very distinctive flavor, so they're often overlooked by mushroom hunters. They come in a variety of sizes and colors. The inside and the outside of a cup are often two different shades or colors.

Coral/Fan-Like Fungi

The mushrooms of this type are the most plant-like in appearance. They can look like little scraps of seaweed, coral, or even jellyfish growing out of mossy logs instead of on the ocean floor. Some look a lot like cauliflower. Some have bulbous tops that almost look like shiny little caps, but they don't have an underside.

No known mushrooms of this type will kill you, but there are several that can wreak havoc on your digestive system.

Polypore and Crust Fungi

Mushrooms of this type come in a variety of shapes and sizes. What they have in common is a tough, dry texture that is often wood-like, leathery, or rubbery. Some grow on the trunks of trees while others grow on the forest floor. Some have caps and stipes. Others look like shelves or hooves growing from the trunks of trees. Some simply grow in shapeless patches or sheets.

Puffballs and Earthballs

What sets these mushrooms apart is the fact that they produce their spores internally instead of on the outer surface of the fruiting body the way other types of mushrooms do.

Puffballs are edible if you catch them in time. While they're young, they have an internal texture similar to marshmallows. They toughen and dry out as they mature. By the time they're ready to release their spores, the outer membrane becomes thin, delicate, and easily torn open.

Warning: Before eating puffballs, always cut them down the middle to make sure you aren't dealing with an earthball in disguise.

Earthballs look a lot like puffballs, but they're not remotely related. In fact, if you cut earthballs open you can see that they contain a distinct cap and stipe like their closer relatives, the boletes.

Truffles and Truffle-Like Fungi

Like puffballs, truffles and truffle look-alikes produce spores internally instead of anywhere on the surface of the mushroom. The two main differences between truffles and puffballs are that truffles fruit underground instead on surfaces, and they don't get torn open or explode to spread their spores. Since they can't distribute their spores on the wind, they depend on animals to sniff them out, dig them up, eat the mushrooms and then deposit the spores elsewhere in the forest.

The most sought-after truffles are native to Europe and haven't successfully been introduced to North American forests, but there are three known species native to California and Oregon. There are also three species of false truffles in the same region.

Truffles and false truffles look very similar on the outside, and both produce complex aromas. When you cut open a truffle, you find a dense labyrinth of wrinkled tubes. False truffles are sometimes gelatinous inside, and sometimes woody and firm.

Jellies

A few types of fungi produce gelatinous blob-like fruiting bodies that look like they've oozed out of whatever surface they're growing from – a log, a tree, or some other mushroom. Many are orange or yellow, some are brown or white. They can have brain-like or frilly surface textures, or they may be smooth. A few have a little bit of a stipe. Where most mushrooms produce spores in a specific location, such as the gills or pores under the cap, jellies release spores from their entire surfaces.

Jellies don't look very appetizing, and few species are recognized as edible. Wood ears, also known as jelly ears, are an exception. Native to Asia, they grow out of the trunks of living elder trees and are popular in traditional Chinese Cuisine.

A Few Other Non-Conformists

Once you start foraging, you're bound to come across mushrooms that don't quite fit into any of the above categories. Fungi evolve rapidly, and they've been around long enough that there are literally thousands of genetic lines. We humans are discovering new species all the time (maybe the next new mushroom will be found by you!) but we just can't keep up.

Some look like gilled mushrooms, but they seem to have evolved to spread their spores some other way and the gills you see are only residual, so you won't be able to get a spore print.

Some only grow as parasites that feed on other species of mushroom. The lobster mushroom is a prime example. It grows around the body of its host and envelops it, so that when you cut it open you find the shriveled remains of the host mushroom inside. These mushrooms are commonly found at farmers' markets in the Pacific Northwest. You would think, since the host mushroom inside can't be properly identified, that more caution would be in order, but lobster mushroom enthusiasts insist that lobster mushrooms never prey upon poisonous mushrooms, and no known poisonings from eating lobster mushrooms have ever been reported.

And then there are the bird's nest fungi, which could be considered a type of cup fungus except that inside the cups you will find tiny "eggs" attached to the center of the cup by fine mycelial threads. When it's time for the mushroom to release its spores, the eggs are ejected from the nest.

Rules of Thumb

Avoid mushrooms with any of these features:

- White gills
- Red coloring on the cap or stem

- Scaley caps
- Rings and /or volva

Not all mushrooms that have white gills or scaley caps are poisonous, but if you avoid them while you are just starting out, you will greatly reduce your risk of getting sick. If you read my first book "Master the World of Edible Wild Plants", you'll remember the concept of the porcupine myth. Never eat anything unless you are 100% certain that it's safe.

Next time you come across a mushroom in the forest, examine it and notice its features. Does it have a cap? Gills? If it has a stipe, what shape is it? Is there evidence of a veil? Cut it down the middle. What do its insides tell you?

If your specimen has gills or pores, practice making a spore print or two. If you like the result, you can even laminate it or lacquer it and keep it as a bookmark or wall art.

In the next chapter, you will find a comprehensive field guide to some of the most popular and easily identified edible mushrooms.

Talk Like a Mushroom

"Communication leads to community, that is, to understanding, intimacy and mutual valuing."
— **Rollo May**

Did you know that mushrooms talk to each other?

Together, they create an underground network known as *mycelium*. Research indicates they send electric signals to each other through this network – much like the signals we receive through the nervous system.

This communication system provides a way for mushrooms to communicate and react to the environment around them. It's still unknown exactly what they're communicating, but researchers suggest that they're exchanging information about the changes in their environment and the availability and quality of resources – essentially, they're sharing reviews for the benefit of the whole community.

And that's what I'd like to ask for your help with now. Foraging for mushrooms is incredibly rewarding, but it requires good knowledge and understanding of what you're doing – otherwise, it can be a dangerous game. So, it's my mission to ensure safe and clear guidance is available to as many would-be mushroom foragers as possible… and that's where you come in.

By leaving a review of this book on Amazon, you'll signpost the information beginner mushroom foragers need to ensure their experience is safe and rewarding.

Simply by letting other readers know how this book has benefitted you and what they can expect from it, you'll point them in the direction of the information they need to forage with confidence and safety.

Thank you for joining me on my mission. When we work together, we can create a network as effective as the mycelium… and what better model of community is there than that?

CHAPTER SIX
Field Guide to Common Edible Mushrooms

Easy Pickings

From the common white button mushroom to the elusive and highly sought-after morel, the United States is home to a wide variety of mushrooms. The sheer number of different types can be overwhelming. But don't worry, I've narrowed it down for you.

This chapter contains two sections. For absolute beginners, the first section describes the top six most foolproof mushrooms that you will ever come across. Not only are they delicious and easy to find, but they're also the easiest varieties to differentiate from those that could make you sick. Without further ado, they are:

- Giant puffballs
- Chicken of the woods
- Hen of the woods
- Dryad's saddle
- Hedgehog Mushrooms
- Beefsteak Mushrooms

If you've purchased the paperback copy of this book, you'll find black and white photos here. However, I've provided free access to the digital book so that you can still easily access color versions of all the same photos. Simply scan this QR code with your phone's camera and enjoy. I apologize, but as a small independent publisher, the print cost for color pictures in a paperback book would eat my entire profit margin. I assure you; digital pictures are advantageous as you can zoom in to a more crisp image than can exist on paper.

Always keep in mind, the field of mycology is ever changing and advancing. Just because a toxic lookalike is not currently known DOES NOT MEAN THERE ISN'T ONE. There is still much to discover in the world of mushrooms so you will forage and identify at your own risk. I cannot guarantee that the accuracy in these pages will remain accurate as this field of study continues to develop.

Giant Puffballs (Calvatia gigantea)

Identification: With a white, spongy exterior, and a creamy white interior, giant puffballs are one of the easiest mushrooms to identify. These mushrooms grow in large clusters in fields, meadows, and other grassy areas. They always grow directly out of the ground, and sometimes grow in fairy rings. They are usually between 4 and 27 inches in diameter.

Range: Puffballs can be found all over the US. They're most commonly found in the Northeast, the North Central States, and the Midwest.

Season: Puffballs fruit in late summer and early fall.

Pictured Lookalike: A very young Death Cap (Amanita phalloides)

Lookalikes: Puffballs do not have a stipe, cap or gills. To make sure you're not dealing with an immature death cap that's still shrouded in its veil, slice each mushroom down the middle. If it has a cap and stipe inside, don't eat it! Death caps are among the deadliest mushrooms in the world. To be safe, you can stay away from very small puffballs. Once a death cap exceeds a couple inches, it could never be mistaken for a puff ball, as puff balls do not have a stipe.

Pictured Lookalike: Earth Ball Scleroderma citrinum, areolatum, verrucosum

Earthballs are another type of poisonous mushroom sometimes misidentified as puffballs. They have a darker, coarse, cracked surface, and look somewhat like a potato. The most blatant way to spot an earthball is to simply cut it open. They have a distinctly dark brown/purple to black interior, completely unlike the full white interior of a puff ball. They cause nausea, vomiting, and diarrhea.

Preparation: Giant puffballs are best eaten when they're harvested young and prepared fresh. They are at their peak when their coloring is bright white, and their texture is creamy and soft. When cooked, they have a mild, earthy flavor that goes well with a variety of dishes. For a decadent treat, try battering them and frying them in oil.

Chicken of the Woods (Laetiporus species)

Identification: This is the number one easiest mushroom to find and identify, as long as you're in the right location. Chicken of the woods grow in clumps on the trunks of dead and dying trees. These polypores have distinctive bright yellow-orange coloring in concentric zones that makes them pretty easy to spot. Instead of a cap and stipe, they have a ruffled shape. When you pick them, you will notice that they have a soft, spongy texture. They have no gills, tiny pores, and a fleshy tender stem. Several different varieties of this species have been identified from region to region – some with a smoother or woodier texture, some with variations on the bright orange coloring. Some have a creamy white underside.

Range: Chicken of the woods is most commonly found east of the continental divide, but they can be found in most mature deciduous forests across the country.

Season: In most areas, these mushrooms appear between August and November.

Lookalikes: There are several lookalikes to chicken of the woods such as the Jack'O Lantern mushroom(has gills), the sulfur shelf mushroom(gives off a faint odor of garlic or onions), hairy stareum(hairy cap and lack of pores), black staining polypore(black, fibrous stem that is not edible), and the giant polypore(round, irregular pores that exude black liquid when squeezed).

Preparation: Chicken of the woods gets its name from its texture and flavor rather than its appearance. This is a hearty, meaty mushroom. is best eaten when it is young and still has a soft, spongy texture. When cooked, it has a mild, nutty flavor. It can be sautéed, grilled, or even fried.

Hen of the Woods (Grifola frondose)

Pictured: Young Hen of the Woods

Identification: It can be easy to mix up the names, but hen of the woods looks very different from chicken of the woods. This is a polypore with a firm texture and a more regular shape, with layers of curved caps that look a bit like the tailfeathers of a hen. The color is a deep brown. Clusters of this mushroom grow on the roots and stumps of mature trees. They can grow to up to fifty pounds, but most specimens you find will be much more modest in size. I've included pictures of both young and mature hen of the woods to show how it ages.

Pictured: Mature Hen of the Woods

Range: Hen of the woods are most common in Japan, where they're known as Maitake. In the United States, they are found most often at the base of oak trees in northern temperate forests.

Season: In many areas, this mushroom can appear in late summer, but sometimes it waits until later in the fall to show up.

Lookalikes: No known poisonous mushrooms bear a resemblance to this distinctive fungus, making it a popular trophy for beginning foragers, but always keep in mind, certainty is key.

It can be difficult to distinguish from the less common black-staining polypore, which looks very similar and grows in the same types of habitat. The underside of black-staining polypore will bruise black or very dark when you press your finger into it. That is the quickest and easiest way to tell them apart.

Preparation: Hen of the Woods is best eaten when it is young and still has a firm, meaty texture. When cooked, it has a savory, earthy flavor that goes well with just about anything. For a satisfying snack, fry them in oil until they're crisp.

Dryad's Saddle (Polyporus squamosus)

Identification: Also known as pheasant back mushrooms, dryad's saddles grow out of the bark of stumps, fallen logs, and living hardwood trees. When you see them on living trees, they're usually pretty low to the ground. This polypore deepens to a deep orange-brown color as it matures. It sports an appealing textured pattern of dark scales on the top surface and is attached to its host by a short, thick stem. They have no gills, but rather are porous on the underside and can smell of watermelon rinds. These mushrooms can get up to two feet in diameter but you will want to harvest them long before they reach that size. They get pretty tough and leathery as they age.

Range: These mushrooms are pretty ubiquitous. They have been found on just about every continent, and they've even been spotted in Australia!

Season: You're most likely to find this mushroom in April and May.

Lookalikes: Dryad's saddle does not have any known poisonous lookalikes. It does look vaguely similar to trainwreckers and giant sawgills, both of which are rare and edible.

Preparation: Dryad's Saddle is best eaten when it is young and still has a firm, meaty texture. If it's difficult to cut it away from the tree with your knife, you're probably not going to have an easier time trying to eat it. When cooked, this mushroom has a mealy odor, but the flavor is mild and nutty.

Hedgehog Mushrooms (Hydnum repandum)

Identification: You can find hedgehog mushrooms growing on the ground in wooded areas. They usually grow in clusters and have a honey brown or creamy brown color. What's distinctive about these mushrooms is that they have long teeth instead of gills or pores, giving them the nickname "sweet tooth" mushrooms. Their texture is soft and spongy. Their orange caps have an irregular shape instead of being perfectly round, and the stipes are sometimes a little off-center.

Range: These mushrooms grow under conifer trees on both the east and west coasts.

Season: Closer to the East Coast, most hedgehogs fruit in summer and early fall. On the West Coast, you're more likely to find them in early spring and late fall. They do pop up anywhere in between though, so keep your eyes peeled!

Lookalikes: You might come across Hydnellums, which look very similar but have a darker color and a tough texture that makes them unfit to eat – unless you feel like chewing on leather. Phellodons are also darker and have a cork-like texture. Their stipes are short to non-existent. Sistotrema confluens, a toothed polypore that was just recently discovered, could be mistaken for hedgehogs except that they grow on tree trunks while hedgehogs only grow out of the ground.

Preparation: Hedgehogs are usually sweet and nutty with a meaty texture, but they do vary in taste. About fifty different species of hedgehogs have been identified around the world, with about twenty found in North America. Some of those varieties can be pretty bitter. The only way to know for sure whether they're suitable for cooking is to place a tiny piece of a cap on your tongue and see how it tastes. If it's bitter, spit it out and compost it. If it's not bitter, spit it out anyway because you don't want to eat it raw. But you can cook the rest of that mushroom! They are related to chanterelles, and cooking with them is very similar. I like to use them as a substitute for chicken in stir fry dishes.

Beefsteak Fungus (Fistulina hepatica)

Identification: I'm including beefsteak mushrooms on this list because they are so distinctive, that it's pretty much impossible to get them confused with any other mushroom. They are a little more difficult to find though. They primarily grow near the base of dying or dead oak trees, and sometimes they're found on chestnut trees.

This deep red polypore looks for all the world like a slab of meat or a tongue (it's sometimes called ox tongue fungus or tongue mushroom) sticking out of its host tree's bark. When you press your thumb into them, they even ooze a blood-like substance. The pores are off-white, tiny and round, and they bruise red/brown.

Range: Beefsteaks are not as common in North America as they are in Europe. The best region to look for them is in the Rocky Mountains.

Season: They are most common in late summer, and they can also be found into early fall.

Lookalikes: No other known polypores have this mushroom's distinctive color.

Preparation: Beefsteaks are delicious if you cook them right. If you don't cook them long enough though, they can be pretty sour and tough. You really can eat it like a steak. I like to cut them into thin slices and grill them or sear them in a pan. You can also fry the meat like bacon or marinate it and make it into jerky.

For the Discerning Gourmand

Once you get more comfortable with your skills identifying mushrooms, taste is going to be just as important as ease of identification. That's why I've rounded up the top five most delicious wild mushrooms you can find from coast to coast:

- Chanterelles
- Morels
- King boletes
- Oyster mushrooms
- Black Trumpets

Chanterelles (Cantharellus genus)

Identification: Chanterelles are one of the most sought-after mushrooms due to their unique flavor and colorful appearance. These mushrooms have a bright yellow color and an apricot or pumpkin-like aroma. They can be enjoyed cooked or raw and make a great addition to salads or pasta dishes. These meaty mushrooms grow in dispersed clusters near the base of a variety of different conifers and hardwood trees. There are several species of chanterelles, and each has a preference for the types of trees they like to partner with. Most of the chanterelles you will see are golden yellow, but some species are white or reddish. Their cap, underside, and stipe are usually all the same color.

These mushrooms usually grow from two to four inches tall. They feel dense and heavy in your hand, rather than light and airy like a lot of other mushrooms that grow out of the ground. The cap is flat at first, then takes on the shape of a funnel. As the mushroom ages the edges curl and become wavy or lobed. The stem is continuous with the cap, solid, smooth and paler at the base. The flesh is firm and the inside is white when cut open.

One of the most critical identifying features chanterelles have is the false gills you will find under their caps instead of true gills or spores. These false gills look like wrinkles or ridges that run down the stem. Instead of forming smooth, straight lines like most gills do, the false gills of chanterelles are wavy and forked like tree branches.

Range: The best places to look for chanterelles are in places where the ground has been disturbed in mixed forests. They are easiest to find along the edges of trails and dirt roads and in areas that have recently been washed out.

Season: These mushrooms are a little more unpredictable than most. Starting in late summer or early fall, avid chanterelle hunters will start casually combing their favorite spots, waiting to see these bright orange caps emerge, looking like bright, shiny egg yolks splattered on the forest floor. The best time to go looking is several days after good, heavy rain. Chanterelles can fruit late into the fall in temperate climates.

Lookalikes: Chanterelles do have some poisonous lookalikes, so pay close attention!

Pictured Lookalike: Jack o' lanterns (Omphalotus olearius), which can cause severe abdominal pain and diarrhea, have true gills instead of the false gills you will find on chanterelles. Jack o' lanterns tend to grow in dense clumps, while chanterelles prefer to spread out. Jack o' lanterns always grow from rotting wood, which is sometimes deceptively buried by forest litter, chanterelles always grow from the ground. Jacks are often funnel shaped at maturity. Chanterelles usually aren't.

Jack mushrooms have true gills, while chanterelles have veins, or false gills. Jack o' lanterns tend to have a thick, fleshy, curving stem and are usually much larger than chanterelles, often 2-3 times larger at maturity.

Pictured Lookalike: False chanterelles (Hygrophoropsis aurantiaca) aren't poisonous, but they don't taste good either. Especially in an area where the amount you can pick is limited, you don't want to end up filling your sack with false chanterelles only to get home and find out they're not edible.

While true chanterelles have false gills, false chanterelles have true gills. The gills of false chanterelles are fine, deep, and close together. Like the false gills of the true chanterelles, the gills of the false chanterelles run down the stipe. False chanterelles have fuzzy caps with darker centers, while true chanterelles are smoother and more uniform in color.

Pictured Lookalike: Wooly chanterelles (Turbinellus floccosus), also sometimes called Scaley Vases, are easy to confuse with older chanterelles. This mushroom is considered edible in some regions of the world, but I've heard enough reports of gastrointestinal distress that I personally wouldn't bother with it.

As chanterelles age, their slightly domed caps become more convex so that they take on the shape of an elegant vase. Wooly chanterelles start out with a convex cap. To add to the confusion, both wooly chanterelles and the real thing like to fruit in the same types of environments and in similar conditions.

The most visible differences between the two are seen on the top of the cap and the stipe. Both have false gills, but the false gills of woolly chanterelles run all the way down and cover the entire stipe, whereas the false gills of chanterelles only extend a little way down the stipe.

Pictured Lookalike: Yellow amanitas (Amanita gemmate) have a similar color to chanterelles. Fortunately, that's about the only similarity, because they can be fatal. Going from the top of the cap to the base of the stipe, there are a number of key differences that are easy to spot:

- Mature yellow amanitas usually have obvious remnants of the veil that covered their caps when they were forming. Dried flecks of the veil stuck to the top of the cap look like little scabs or scales.

- Yellow amanitas have white gills that don't connect to the stipe, where chanterelles have false gills that are usually the same color as the rest of the mushroom and run down the stipe.

- Yellow amanitas have a long, slender stipe with a little skirt, which is another remnant of the veil.

- The base of a yellow amanita's stipe is bulbous. Chanterelles stipes aren't necessarily uniform or straight, but they don't have that distinctive bulb.

Preparation: Chanterelles are delicious any way you prepare them. Slice them up and sauté them in butter with vegetables, add them to your spaghetti sauce, or drop them into a pot of soup. I know that some people nibble on raw chanterelles and mix them into salads, but I wouldn't recommend it. Even non-toxic mushrooms can be difficult to digest if they're not fully cooked.

Morels (Morchella genus)

Identification: First, I have to warn you that the challenge of hunting morels is downright addictive. People get pretty obsessed come spring when the weather is just right. It may take a few diligent scouting expeditions before you find your first, but when you do you will be hooked.

Morel mushrooms are most commonly associated with elm trees, but they can also be found under cottonwoods, ash trees, and sycamores, as well as around old apple orchards.

Morels grow out of the ground and tend to blend in with the background, so they can be pretty hard to spot. Their oblong caps are covered with wrinkles in a mesh-like pattern with deep pits. When you cut them open, they're completely hollow on the inside, from the top of the cap to the end of the stipe. These distinctive mushrooms are pretty easy to identify if you can find one.

Range: Morels can be found in every region, from California to the New York Islands, as Woody Guthrie would say. They typically grow in moist, well-drained soils in areas with partial shade. South-facing hillsides that have a lot of sun exposure are also a good place to search for morels. The season following a wildfire often yields an abundant crop of morels, which is why it's not uncommon for morel enthusiasts to start collecting burn scar maps as spring approaches. Sites with windblown trees and logged-out areas are also prime morel hunting spots.

Season: Morels can appear as early as February in warmer climates. In Alaska, don't expect them to show up until later in the spring.

Pictured Lookalike: False morel (Gyromitra esculenta)

Lookalikes: There are morels, and then there are false morels. Some say false morels are edible if you cook them just right, but if you don't, they can make you pretty sick. Personally, I wouldn't take the chance. Fun fact: the toxin they contain is used in rocket fuel. There have been no immediate deaths from eating them, but we can only speculate on the long-term effects.

One of the easiest ways to tell the difference between a true morel and a false one is that true morels are hollow inside. Before you pick a mushroom and slice it open though, you can usually tell a false morel by the irregular shape of its cap. False morels have lobes or waves, or they bulge outwards, or they can look squashed down. Their caps hang freely from the stipe, as opposed to the fully attached caps of true morels.

Preparation: Entire cookbooks have been written about the endless possibilities with morel mushrooms. Dozens of cookbooks, actually. You can get pretty fancy with them, as a number of posh restaurants do. They are amazing in butter sauces and creamy soups. Or you can simply sauté them and have them for breakfast with your eggs and potatoes.

King Boletes (Boletus edulis)

Identification: King boletes, also known as porcini, steinpilz, cep, penny bun, or simply "the king," only grow out of the ground, never out of trees or logs. They are most commonly found under fir, spruce, pine, hemlock, and other conifer trees. The mushroom cap will look like a slightly greasy bun when you look down on it. The color can range from yellow-brown to a reddish brown. The underside of the cap has sponge-like, rounded pores that are white when young and yellow-olive when mature. The tubes are sunken around the stalk. The flesh is generally white all around, but occasionally has some yellow stains near the base of the stalk.

These mushrooms are hefty. Their caps can grow as large as 10 inches in diameter, and they can weigh over a pound. The stipes are thick and bulgy, and sometimes every bit as big as the caps. In some species, sections of the stipe can be peeled away like string cheese.

King boletes spoil quickly once they reach maturity. They are popular among forest creatures and insects as well as humans, so if you want to find a healthy, appetizing specimen that has not already been munched on, you've got some competition.

Range: These meal-size mushrooms can be found in woodlands and forests throughout the northern hemisphere.

Season: The best time to find these mushrooms is in late summer. In warm and temperate climates, they can appear as late as October.

Pictured Lookalike: Bitter Bolete (Tylopilus felleus)

Lookalikes: There are numerous species of boletes, but none of them are as tasty as the king. Bitter boletes look the most similar to king boletes. Their pores are pinkish instead of white and the stipe is covered by what looks like dark brown netting. Like king boletes, bitter boletes also get pretty big.

To tell the difference between the king and its less desirable relatives, keep in mind these key features:

- The flesh of the king is white and it doesn't leave a stain. The pores don't stain either.
- The stipe is always white or tannish, never yellow or purple.
- The top of the stipe has a fine, net-like pattern. On some kings, this pattern extends to the bottom of the stipe.

Preparation: When cooked, King Boletes have a savory, earthy flavor that goes well with a variety of dishes. I like to slice them, dip them in beaten eggs, coat them with seasoned breadcrumbs, and fry them. You can also add them to soups, stews, and sauces or layer grilled slices over a bed of rice or mashed potatoes.

Oyster Mushrooms (Pleurotus ostreatus)

Identification: Oyster mushrooms are another delicious treat that is easy to identify. They fruit on dead and dying trees, on fallen logs, and on stumps. They have an oyster or fan-shaped cap that is usually tan or brown. Oysters are usually around two to ten inches in diameter, but they can get much bigger. You will often find them growing in clusters like bouquets.

Oyster mushrooms have a thick stipe that can vary in length and is often curved. The gills are broad and fairly spaced. Some of the gills run all the way down the stipe, while others only run partially down. The cap is smooth. Most oyster mushrooms are white or light brown. They smell a bit like licorice.

Range: These delicacies can be found in temperate regions all over the world. They can also be found in the Southeastern states where it's warm and humid.

Season: Oyster mushrooms generally fruit during the late summer and early fall. In warmer climates, they can keep popping up into the winter months.

Lookalikes: There are a few different varieties of oysters and oyster-like mushrooms. Some taste better than others.

Pictured Lookalike: Angel wing (Pleurocybella porrigens)

However, this mushroom does have one poisonous lookalike, the angel wing. This is a mushroom that we believed was perfectly safe up until 2004, when it killed seventeen people out of 59 that it sickened in Japan. The angel wing contains a highly unstable amino acid that was likely the culprit in those tragedies, plus an additional death in 2009. As you have probably gleaned by now, mushroom foraging is not for the faint of heart. Things change, sometimes unpredictably. Always use caution.

Poisonous angel wings grow in the same conditions and regions as oysters do, so it's very important to know how to tell them apart. Angel wings have thinner caps that are indented in the middle and turned up around the edges, like wings in flight. They are sometimes shaped like funnels. Angel wings do tend to be very white or even ivory while oyster mushrooms have a much grayer hue. Angel wings also tend to not have stems but rather sprout directly from the tree with a stubby growth. Taking a spore print may or may not help you tell the difference between oysters and angel wings. Both produce white prints, but oyster spores are sometimes grayish.

Preparation: These versatile mushrooms have a mild flavor and a firm texture that holds up to a variety of cooking methods. Because these mushrooms are grown commercially as well as found in the wild, they show up on a lot of restaurant menus and are often featured as substitutes for meat in vegetarian dishes. They can even be pickled.

Black Trumpets (Cantharellaceae genus)

Identification: Black trumpets are an elusive forest prize if you can find them. Walk slowly, looking more or less straight down, paying close attention to damp, dark areas such as patches of thick moss. If you see one, stay in that area and look around for more! They usually grow in clusters.

You are looking for black or brown funnel-shaped mushrooms with wavy edges that roll outward. The inside of the cap (top of the funnel) will usually have small scales. The underside is smooth – no gills, pores or teeth. The stipe, usually a few inches tall, can be slightly lighter than the cap, but it's usually the same color. The inside of the stipe is hollow and the flesh breaks easily.

Range: These treasures are found in damp and humid hardwood forests in temperate regions all over the world. Their favorite trees to partner with are oak and beech.

Season: Black trumpets typically fruit during the summer and fall months, and in some areas, like central California, they can fruit through the winter.

*Pictured Lookalike: Devil's Urn (**Urnula criterium**)*

Lookalikes: Black trumpets may be confused with the devil's urn, another small, black cup-like mushroom that grows on the forest floor. The edges of devil's urns are thinner and tend to roll slightly inward instead of outward. They tend to look more like goblets than a trumpet. However, don't let the name scare you – they're not poisonous.

Preparation: When you cook with these black trumpets, you don't need to dress them up too much. They have a rich, smoky flavor that stands on its own. They are excellent when paired with fresh-caught fish.

Shaggy Manes (Coprinus comatus)

Identification: Shaggy manes are one of the few species of mushrooms that enjoy sunshine. They can be found in grassy areas with rich soil, and they also fruit in areas where the ground has recently been disturbed.

Sporting a style all their own, shaggy manes have a long, slender cap with scales that curl upward. When young, shaggy many caps have a cylindrical bullet shape with upturned tan to reddish-brown scales. Their caps are generally 2 to 6 inches tall and 1 to 2 inches wide, becoming more bell-shaped as they age. Shaggy manes stems are hollow and white to light tan in color with a partial veil. Cut the stem near ground level and you should see a hollow tube leading up under the cap. Additionally, if you cut open a young shaggy mane, you'll see its white gills packed together tightly.

As shaggy manes mature, the gills turn pink and then transform from the inside out into a black, inky goo that melts away. Make sure you get them while they're young. As soon as the inky goo starts to bleed through, they're too far gone to pick.

Range: Shaggy manes can be found across North America. They're particularly common in the Northeast and Midwest. Golf courses, city parks, front lawns and the edges of trails are great places to look for shaggy manes. They usually fruit in large groups, sometimes scattered and sometimes close together.

Season: These are fall mushrooms. Look for them about two days after the first fall rain in regions where precipitation is seasonal.

Lookalikes: Inky cap is a lookalike that causes severe reactions when consumed with alcohol. It's pretty easy to tell them apart once you know what to look for, but just to be on the safe side I would caution against drinking while you are eating or digesting shaggy manes. Inky caps dissolve into black ink the way shaggy manes do, but before that happens, the surfaces of their caps is grey instead of white and lacks scales. As long as you are not consuming alcohol, inky caps are every bit as edible as shaggy manes.

Pictured Lookalike: False parasols (Chlorophyllum molybdites) or green spored parasols, commonly nicknamed the vomiter (you can probably guess why), are another species of mushroom that are white with brown scales on the surface of the cap. The main difference is that they are round and wide instead of tall and slender. These mushrooms do not dissolve into goo the way shaggy manes do.

Preparation: However you decide to cook these, do it right away! Shaggy manes do not keep. Put them in your fridge raw or leave them on the counter for a few hours, and you will have a mess on your hands. They contain a lot of water, and so they're best when used in soups and stews.

Lobster Mushrooms (Hypomyces lactifluorum)

Identification: Although they are a fungus, lobster mushrooms are not the type that produce their own fruiting bodies. Instead, they cannibalize other species of mushrooms, completely transforming them, and use those hosts to distribute their own spores. Now that you know you're not looking for your everyday mushroom, but rather one that has been transformed and distorted, these monstrosities (which taste far better than they look) will be easier for you to identify.

The easy-to-identify lobster mushroom has an almost shell-like vivid orange or red surface surrounding the converted host mushroom. They are coated with a fine layer of bumps. The two species of mushrooms that lobsters cannibalize have your average caps, gills and stipes, but these are usually obscured. You may or may not see wrinkly evidence of the host mushroom's former gills. Avoid lobster mushrooms that have turned purple as they are no longer suitable for sonsumption.

Range: The mushrooms that lobsters cannibalize grow mostly in conifer forests. They can be found under cedars and Douglas firs, growing from under loose forest floor material. They are particularly easy to find in the Pacific Northwest.

Season: Inland lobster season runs from late July into October.

Lookalikes: The only mushrooms you might confuse these with would be chanterelles. The coloring is similar, and the trace of gills that you can see in a lobster's shape can sometimes look like the false gills of a chanterelle. If you're not sure, cut the mushroom open. Lobster mushrooms are white inside, while chanterelles are orange all the way through.

Preparation: Lobster mushrooms are highly sought-after for their savory, lobster-like flavor and firm texture.

Familiarize yourself with the mushrooms in this chapter, and you will have the knowledge you need to fill your basket with confidence. Simply focus on the mushrooms that you can verify are edible and ignore anything about which you're not 100% sure.

In the next chapter, I'll go over the poisonous mushrooms that are most commonly mistaken for benign lookalikes. You might be surprised (and relieved!) to see that it's a pretty short list.

CHAPTER SEVEN
Ferocious Fungi

Mushroom poisoning is nothing to be cavalier about. Even though most cases don't result in death, the effects can be debilitating and long-lasting, ranging from mild stomach cramps to complete kidney failure and permanent brain damage.

The good news is that you can manage the risks very effectively simply by doing some due diligence and familiarizing yourself with the most common poisonous mushrooms and their lookalikes. Only about three percent of all known mushroom species are poisonous, and of those three percent, only ten percent are potentially deadly, so it's not an overwhelming amount of information that you need to commit to memory.

Ten to Watch Out For

The top ten poisonous mushrooms you want to be aware of are:

- The False Parasol
- The Death Cap
- The Destroying Angel
- False Morel
- Funeral Bell
- Fool's Webcap
- Common Conecap
- Fly Agarics

False Parasol (chlorophyllum molybdites)

The false parasol, also known as the green spored parasol or vomiter, is eaten more often than any other species of poisonous mushroom in the United States. False parasols grow readily in lawns and gardens, often in fairy rings. They look pretty and they taste okay, or so I've heard, but the vomiting and diarrhea can last for several hours (probably not worth it).

One reason people eat these mushrooms is because, as discussed before, they look a bit similar to shaggy manes, which is another species that pops up in lawns and gardens, sometimes in a ring formation. The key difference is that the caps of false parasols are round and wide, where the caps of shaggy manes hug the stipe and are long and slender.

Another key difference is that Shaggy manes start to disintegrate into a black goo shortly after being picked. They are quite delicate. False parasols, on the other hand, look delicate but they have a firm, meaty texture not unlike that of the mushrooms you find at the grocery store, which may account for the decision people occasionally make to nibble on them.

The effects of eating false parasols disprove several common myths that people unfortunately go by when trying to figure out whether a mushroom is edible. Some common myths I've heard are:

- All white mushrooms are safe to eat (False!)

- Any mushroom is safe to eat when thoroughly cooked (False!)
- Insects avoid poisonous mushrooms (False!)
- All poisonous mushrooms taste bad. (False!)

False parasols break each one of those rules. They are white, they are still poisonous no matter how you cook them, they attract insects, they taste fine, and they will make you vomit. Don't ask for many shortcuts in mushroom foraging my friends.

Death Cap (Amanita phalloides)

Another mushroom to watch out for is the death cap. Worldwide, they cause more deaths each year than any other fungus. These dingy white mushrooms look very ordinary. Like false parasols, they also appear in gardens and lawns.

When this mushroom is mature you can usually see the remnants of its veil as a skirt or ring around the upper stipe and a volva at the base. A newly emerging death cap, with its veil covering the whole cap and stipe, can look like a small puffball. This is why it's important to slice each puffball that you harvest down the middle. If you see a cap and stipe forming inside, don't eat it!

Destroying Angel (Amanita virosa)

This mushroom looks more innocent than its name implies, but it is likely to cause serious harm if you eat it, and it can even be fatal. A distinctive feature of this mushroom is that it is pure white. If you can remember that and avoid eating any mushrooms that are completely devoid of coloring, your foraging expeditions will be that much safer, and you won't be missing out on anything. The common button mushrooms that you can find in the grocery store are also all white, but you're not likely to encounter them in the wild.

False Morel (Gyromitra genus)

The only mushroom you're likely to confuse a false morel with is a true morel. Sometimes called brain mushrooms, false morels are irregular in shape. Their caps often look squashed down as opposed to the upright cone shapes that top true morels. True morels have clearly defined ridges and deep pits, while false morels are less well defined. The vomiting, diarrhea, headaches, and nausea that result shortly after eating false morels can be severe.

Funeral Bell or Autumn Skullcap (Galerina marginata)

These clusters of honey-colored caps contain the same lethal compound that is found in Death Caps, and a single mushroom has enough to kill an adult. They look dangerously similar to the various species of honey mushrooms and Psilocybe cyanescens, a particularly potent species of magic mushrooms, so I would caution you as a beginning forager to avoid anything that vaguely fits the description.

Because they look so similar to honey mushrooms, and because they are so deadly, I don't recommend foraging for honey mushrooms at all until you've had an expert personally show you the difference between honeys and funeral bells.

One of the surest ways to tell whether you've got a funeral bell is to make a spore print. The result will be reddish-brown. Honey mushrooms make white spore prints.

Psilocybe cyanescens also sometimes make brownish spore prints, but their caps have a wavy shape instead of the rounded or flat shape of funeral bell caps, so they are a little easier to tell apart. Still, I would consult with an expert before sampling anything you've identified as this particular species of magic mushroom, which is rumored to be particularly potent.

Fool's Webcap (Cortinarius orellanus)

It's highly unlikely that you will ever come across this meaty little killer in the United States, but if you do, and if you put it in your mouth, you will probably experience flu-like symptoms that begin within a day and linger. Severe cases can eventually result in kidney failure and sometimes death.

Fool's webcap is sometimes mistaken for chanterelles in southern Europe, where it's more common, despite the fact that there are a number of key differences. Fool's webcaps have reddish-brown caps and widely spaced gills that don't run down the stipe. Chanterelles have more of an orange look and shallow false gills that do run part way down the stipe.

Common Conecap or Duncecap (Conocybe genus)

Not all species in the conocybe genus are poisonous, but they should all be treated like they are because they're so difficult to tell apart. In some cases, proper identification requires a microscope. These mushrooms are so small and delicate, they wouldn't be worth the effort anyway unless they were profoundly delicious, which I'm willing to bet they're not.

Conecaps are commonly found growing in lawns, grasslands, dead moss, the dung of cattle and other herbivores, and decaying wood. They mostly pop up during the summer and autumn months. Most of these delicate looking mushrooms have a long, thin fragile stipe and a conical or bell-shaped cap that is usually dark brown. Four species that belong to this family contain the hallucinogenic compounds psilocin and psilocybin. One, which is particularly common as a lawn mushroom, contains the same deadly toxins as the death cap.

To make sure you're not inadvertently putting any of these potential killers in your basket, avoid any mushrooms that fit this description:

- Tiny mushrooms with a cone-shaped cap that ranges in color from off-white to dark brown. Some caps have a yellowish-green center.
- Pale gills that attach to the stipe but don't descend.
- Thin, dainty stem.

Angel Wings (Pleurocybella porrigens)

If you pick up a field guide that was published before 2005, you're likely to read that Angel wings are not only edible, but tasty. We now know that these innocent looking mushrooms are extremely toxic. Symptoms include sub-acute tremor, weakness, difficulty moving, muscle spasms, sometimes complete paralysis, coma, kidney damage, brain damage, and finally death about ten days after the onset of symptoms. The symptoms don't develop until 13 to 18 days after the mushroom is consumed.

Our knowledge of the toxic effects of these mushrooms is based on two incidents in Japan; one in 2004 and one in 2009, where a total of 60 people got sick from eating the mushrooms and eighteen died. All the people who got sick were elderly and had compromised kidney function.

The deaths were a shock to the mushroom world because people had been consuming angel wings for centuries! It's likely that people still eat them, and no further illnesses or deaths have been reported. Were the mushrooms in Japan a new mutation that made them different from the species found everywhere else? Did the tragedies have to do with the ages or physical condition of the victims, or the quantities they consumed? It's still a mystery!

Scientists have isolated a toxin, a highly unstable amino acid that could behave very differently in different environments.

Angel wings can look like oyster mushrooms to the untrained eye. Like oysters, they grow out of dead and dying trees and can be found in temperate forests throughout the Northern Hemisphere. The white caps grow in close clusters and are two to four inches in diameter, and they are shaped like a shell, petal, or fan, just like oysters. The stem is short and very thin.

The main difference between oysters and angel wings is the shape of the cap. Angel wings have thinner caps that slightly curl upward. Their slightly convex shape can make them look like an outstretched tongue, and they sometimes form a funnel. The flesh of the cap is much thinner than that of an oyster mushroom.

Fly Agarics (Amanita muscaria & Amanita pantherine)

Amanita muscaria and amanita pantherine, commonly known fly agarics, are native to the temperate regions of the northern hemisphere. These look similar to the familiar large mushrooms with red spots that are often depicted in the art of psychedelic culture, but these are not the mushrooms you want to eat if you're looking to get high. Instead of the bright solid red caps reminiscent of the smurfs' dwellings, these poisonous cousins have caps that are more of a faded yellowish-orange color. They can cause nausea, vomiting, and other unpleasant effects. They do contain psychoactive compounds as well as toxins, but you're likely going to be too sick to notice if you take the risk.

Some people claim to be able to render the toxins in these mushrooms inert by cooking these mushrooms in a certain way, but if you don't know exactly what you're doing, you're playing with potentially deadly fire. In some cases, you can get sick just from inhaling the fumes from mushrooms while they're cooking!

Deadly Dapperling (Lepiota brunneoincarnata)

Deadly dapperling mushrooms are a common sight in parks and lawns in various regions of Europe and Asia, but they're still rare in the United States. Their pointed caps have a scaly texture. They can be pure white or white at the edge with yellowish, pinkish, or tan centers, and they have a white stipe and gills. Nausea and vomiting usually start ten hours after consumption, and liver damage becomes apparent a few days later.

How To Avoid Mushroom Poisoning

Do not eat any wild mushrooms unless you're 100% sure they are what you think they are. Only select specimens that are young and fresh. Thoroughly familiarize yourself with each mushroom's appearance, habitat, season, and range before you go foraging. Make sure the mushroom meets each of these qualifications before putting them in your basket:

a. **The mushroom was found growing in the expected environment and season.** If you're on the West coast and find something that looks like a chanterelle, but it's suspiciously fruiting in early June, don't pick it!

b. **The habitat is correct.** Any supposed oyster mushroom that's growing out of the ground is not an oyster mushroom, is it? Oysters only grow out of dead and dying trees.

c. **The size, shape, color, and texture are what you would expect.** A chicken of the woods that looks brown or grey would definitely be suspect.

d. **The anatomy is correct**. A king bolete with gills is definitely not a king bolete.

You can expect that in your early days, you're likely to spend a lot of time scrutinizing specimens, shrugging, and returning them to the forest floor. Be patient, and your skills will improve with practice. One day you will be able to spot a morel from yards away! Well, ok, there's probably not a person alive who can do that, but you will get pretty good over time.

Always cook your mushrooms before eating them. This is not a foolproof way to deal with any toxic mushrooms you might have inadvertently harvested. Cooking foods is a way to make foods more digestible, generally speaking, and this is especially true for mushrooms.

If you're about to try a type of mushroom for the first time, only nibble on a small amount (after cooking it!) and wait a full day to see if any symptoms develop. Do this even after you have verified that the mushrooms you've harvested aren't poisonous. Even if you're 110% sure, you still want to rule out the possibility of an allergic reaction.

If You Suspect Mushroom Poisoning

Even when you have taken every possible precaution, there is always a chance that you may still consume poisonous mushrooms. The first symptoms of mushroom poisoning usually show up within one to twenty-four hours. If you feel any unusual gut pain during this time period, drink plenty of water and immediately seek medical attention. Excessive salivation, sweating, tears, and lactation can also be signs of mushroom poisoning. Don't shrug off any drowsiness, visual distortions, or delusions that you experience – these can also be signs of toxicity. Be aware that symptoms can come and go in waves that reoccur even after medical treatment, so don't drop your guard when you start to feel better. You may not be out of the woods yet. Stay vigilant until you're sure that you have fully recovered.

While you may think of mushrooms primarily as wild food, there is more to know about them than that. Read on to find out some intriguing facts about medicinal mushrooms and how they can help keep you fit and healthy.

CHAPTER EIGHT
Mushroom Medicine

Fungi have a long and storied history in medicine. People around the world began using them for healing and wellness thousands of years ago, and many cultures have preserved traditional folk remedies using mushrooms that are hundreds of years old. In traditional Chinese medicine, for example, fungi have been used to treat a variety of ailments including respiratory and gastrointestinal issues. In the West, fungi have been used since ancient times to treat skin conditions and infections. Chaga is a medicinal mushroom that has been used to treat everything from colds to cancer.

These folk remedies are often based on traditional knowledge and anecdotal evidence, rather than scientific studies. However, many of these traditional remedies have recently been found to be effective in clinical studies, and some have even been adopted by modern medicine.

From new therapies derived from mushrooms in labs to remedies that have been handed down through the generations, the medicinal benefits of fungi are hard to ignore. In this chapter, we'll explore some of the ways that you can forage and use wild fungi for your own health and wellness.

In recent years, modern science has begun to study the medicinal properties of mushrooms, and there is now a growing body of evidence showing their potential for treating a wide range of conditions. Several species of mushrooms are now harvested and used in medical treatments for cancer, rheumatoid arthritis, Chron's disease, and other autoimmune disorders. Supplements made from reishi and shiitake mushrooms, delectable edibles in their own right, are popular as immune system boosters.

The vast majority of mushrooms used to produce the medicines you can get at your local pharmacy or health food store are grown in laboratories and farmed. Numerous species of mushrooms only grow in the complex ecosystems found in nature, and so their medicinal properties are still largely untapped.

As a forager, you don't have to wait for the healing power of mushrooms to be processed, packaged, and stocked on the shelves of your local health food store. With appropriate knowledge, you can forage fresh organic mushrooms directly from the forest, ensuring that you get the full and unadulterated health benefits they offer.

Let's take a look at a few medicinal mushrooms that have proven themselves throughout centuries of use and are making new waves in the world of medicine. Some of the most popular medicinal mushrooms are reishi, shiitake, turkey tail, chaga, and maitake. These mushrooms have been used for centuries to treat a variety of ailments, and modern science is now beginning to uncover their healing potential.

Three Common Wild Mushrooms to Keep You Healthy

Chaga (Inonotus obliquus)

Chaga has been used in Russian folk medicine as a treatment for cancer for centuries, and it's also popular in Poland and other Eastern European cultures for treating digestive issues and heart and liver conditions. It's known for its anti-inflammatory, antioxidant, and anticancer properties, as well as its ability to boost the immune system.

The science is a little behind when it comes to crediting this mushroom for its traditional health benefits. It has destroyed cancer cells in petri dishes on several occasions (Chung et al., 2010), but has yet to be tested on living humans.

What has been verified is that tea made from chaga is chock full of antioxidants and important minerals like calcium, magnesium, iron, zinc, and copper, all of which are vital to a healthy immune system. The beta glucans that it contains are known to boost immune functioning. Ounce for ounce, it contains more potassium than a banana. People who drink this tea report that it has a strangely energizing effect and seems to reduce their need for sleep.

Making chaga into tea is the only way to consume it, since biting into the mushroom itself would be like trying to chew on a rock. Reportedly, the tea has a delicious flavor.

Before steeping your chaga, break it into one-inch chunks by wrapping it in a cloth, setting it on a steady surface, and hitting it with a hammer. Pour hot (not quite boiling) water over your chaga and let it steep for a full hour. The brew will be a dark reddish-brown color when it's ready. For an even stronger tea, you can brew it in a crock pot on the lowest setting. You don't need to drink the tea immediately after brewing it. You can keep it in the fridge for several days. Some people use it as a base for smoothies and oatmeal.

This special polypore is typically found growing on birch trees in New England, Eastern Canada, and parts of Russia. It's particularly common in Maine. Chaga is easy to identify due to its hard black shell-like exterior (resembling cracked blackened charcoal) which stands out against the white bark of the birch trees that host it. When you cut it open, the flesh inside ranges from a dark amber to light brown. Only harvest chaga from living trees.

Once chaga begins to fruit, it grows very slowly and takes up to fifteen years to mature, so be sure to forage responsibly and don't take more from the forest than you need.

Because chaga has a high oxalate content, it is not recommended for those prone to kidney stones or kidney disease.

Maitake (Grifola frondosa)

Maitake is the Japanese name of the mushroom commonly called Hen of the Woods in the United States. The name means dancing mushroom. According to legend villagers in feudal times danced for joy whenever they found maitake because they knew they could sell it for a lot of money. Their value was based as much on their exquisite flavor as it was for their medicinal properties. These mushrooms were believed to invigorate the body and contribute to a long life. They are now known for their ability to lower blood sugar, reduce cholesterol, and fight cancer. They also have anti-inflammatory and antioxidant properties. To identify, refer to the previous chapter.

Methods to grow this mushroom were developed commercially in the 1980s, but specimens found in the wild are often much bigger and more robust than the ones you can buy. To make the most of the healing properties this mushroom offers, harvest it when it's young and tender, cook it fresh, and serve it as part of a balanced meal. This is more of a superfood than a medicine, and there are no known side effects. You may want to consult your doctor before eating large quantities if you have diabetes, as they can affect your blood sugar.

Bear's Head (Hericium Americanum)

Bear's head is a tooth mushroom that is closely related to Lion's Mane. Covered with long white spines that turn brown with age, it grows in North America, Europe, and Asia. It prefers hardwoods, either already decomposing or still living. These mushrooms have a mild and sweet flavor that some say is a bit like crab. They contain vitamin D, fiber, iron, several antioxidants, and protein. Early research indicates that it has the potential to inhibit the growth of tumors, lower cholesterol, regulate blood sugar, and protect nerves from damage. Indigenous people in North America developed a method to dry and powder this mushroom and use it to stop bleeding wounds. With potent anti-microbial properties, it's excellent for cleaning wounds as well.

Proceed with Caution and Seek Professional Guidance

It's important to remember that mushrooms can be poisonous, so exercise an abundance of caution when foraging and preparing your own medicines. Before doing so, consult a qualified herbalist or naturopath. They can help you identify the right mushrooms for your needs, as well as provide advice on how to safely prepare and use them.

Please note that the United States FDA does not approve the use of any of the mushrooms described in this chapter in the treatment of any ailments or illnesses. Always seek medical advice from a qualified healthcare professional before consuming medicinal mushrooms. A doctor can help you understand the potential benefits and side effects associated with each mushroom you are interested in trying. It's particularly important to talk to a doctor if you are pregnant, if you have a medical condition, or if you are taking any medications, as medicinal mushrooms can cause interactions.

If you're interested in learning more about the medicinal benefits of fungi, there are a number of resources available. The MycoMedica website provides information about the medicinal properties of many common mushrooms. The National Center for Complementary and Integrative Health also has a wealth of information about the potential health benefits of medicinal mushrooms. In my opinion, it's worth taking time to learn as much as you can about the mycological pharmacy hidden in your local forest. After all, they might save your life someday!

CHAPTER NINE
The Kaleidoscopic Killers

On October 3rd, 1799, a curious occurrence took place in London's Green Park. A man, known to us only as J.S., gathered mushrooms for his family's breakfast, as he did most mornings. An hour later, he began to see black spots and flashes of color. He felt disoriented. He couldn't get up from the table. He couldn't move at all.

His wife complained of stomach cramps, and his daughter complained that her elbows were cold. His eight-year-old son was laughing hysterically and couldn't control himself. J.S. started to suspect the mushrooms were poisonous. When he was finally able to break free of the breakfast table, he ran out into the street to find help.

By the time he found someone to describe the situation to, he had forgotten where he was going and why!

Fortunately, a physician named Everard Brande was passing by, and J.S. convinced him to follow him home, although he still couldn't articulate what was going on. The family's bizarre symptoms came and went in waves. Their eyes would widen and their breathing would become irregular. They all talked about how afraid they were of death, except for the eight-year-old boy who was still laughing. When his parents scolded him, he only spoke gibberish.

Doctor Brande took detailed notes as the events unfolded, wrote up a report, and had it published in a prestigious medical journal for all posterity. That, dear reader, was the first documented mushroom trip in the West. It's little wonder people are so skittish around mushrooms.

Foraging for Magic Mushrooms

Any trip into the forest to forage for mushrooms is exciting because you never know what you'll find. Each mushroom, in my opinion, is fascinating and magical in its own way. If you're up for it, you may be able to find mushrooms that will take you on a completely different type of magical trip that you'll never forget.

While I have never partaken in magic mushrooms myself, I have come across hundreds of the little beauties in the wild, and I am well acquainted with dozens of individuals who consider magic mushroom use a vital and profoundly important part of their lives. I have spoken with them in depth about their experiences, which they are always eager to share. I certainly cannot condone the use of any illegal substance. That being said, if the thought of shaking your reality tree sounds intriguing, read on.

In this chapter, we'll explore the fascinating world of magic mushrooms, their effects, and legal issues surrounding their harvest, possession, and usage. We will focus on the four most common types of magic mushrooms in North America.

What are Magic Mushrooms?

Magic mushrooms, also known as psychedelic mushrooms, are a type of fungi that contain psychoactive compounds like psilocybin. Psilocybin is a hallucinogenic substance that can cause intense visual and auditory hallucinations as well as altered states of consciousness and mood changes.

For generations, people have been using psychoactive mushrooms as a tool to explore the psyche, gain a new perspective on life, and heal from emotional traumas. The effects of consuming magic mushrooms vary from person to person. Your own experiences can vary widely depending on your state of mind, personal situation, the mushrooms you take, and the quantities you ingest. A mushroom trip can range from calming and relaxing to profoundly spiritual or even downright horrifying.

The effects of magic mushrooms can be unpredictable, as the levels of hallucinogenic and psychoactive compounds vary from mushroom to mushroom. So if you choose to partake, you should be ready for anything. It's best to start with a very small amount and slowly work your way up to the level of experience you're looking for.

Alterations to your perception and consciousness will typically start within an hour and can last up to six hours. Within a few hours of swallowing a bite of a magic mushroom, you might experience feelings of euphoria, enhanced sensory perception, or a sense of connectedness with nature that are the hallmarks of a mushroom trip done right. The visual distortions, giddiness, and euphoria that often lasts several hours can be an enticing offer. Many report feeling deeply peaceful, transcendent, and connected but disengaged. This is a useful space to be if you want to make an objective assessment of your situation under the guidance of a trained psychotherapist. However, if the dosage is too high, distorted thought patterns can interfere with this experience and even lead to panic and paranoia.

Magic mushrooms taste notoriously awful, so most people ingest them in teas or put them in food to disguise the flavor rather than eating them straight. Magic mushrooms also keep very well after they've been dehydrated.

Are Magic Mushrooms Safe?

It's important to note that magic mushrooms are not without risks, and they're not for everyone. As with any drug, it's crucial to be aware of the potential side effects and safety precautions. If you're considering using magic mushrooms, you definitely want to speak with a medical professional and an experienced psychedelic practitioner first. They can help you understand the potential risks and how to use them responsibly.

The most common negative side effects associated with magic mushrooms are dizziness, drowsiness, loss of physical coordination, impaired concentration, muscle weakness, unusual physical sensations, nausea, vomiting, and traumatic hallucinations that can have a lasting effect on a person's psyche. I have heard stories of individuals who were never the same after having a bad trip. This is definitely a *partake-at-your-own-risk* type of situation.

Legal Precautions for Foraging and Eating Magic Mushrooms

Many species of magic mushrooms are illegal in the United States and most other countries. It's important to become familiar with the laws of the area you're in and make sure you're not putting yourself at risk of breaking those laws.

It's also important to be aware of the potential legal risks associated with ingesting magic mushrooms. It can be difficult to prove that you haven't ingested any illegal substances, so it's important to be aware of the potential repercussions if you're caught tripping. Considering the title of this book, I presume the majority of readers would like to avoid that under most circumstances.

The Most Common Magic Mushrooms in North America

The four types of magic mushrooms that are most commonly foraged in North America are colloquially known as gold caps, liberty caps, wavy caps, and flying saucers. These innocent-looking little brown mushrooms are all close cousins, belonging to the Psilocybe genus, so they share a lot of identifying features.

Several deadly species look similar to magic mushrooms, so it's important to make a positive identification when foraging. Psilocybes all:

- Bruise blue when squeezed or pressed
- Have caps that are less than four inches in diameter

- Have gills that attach to the stipe

- Have brownish caps that darken and become sticky when wet

- Fruit in the fall and winter, usually following a steep drop in temperature

- Produce dark purplish-brown or purplish-black spore prints

If your mushroom doesn't have all of these characteristics, check to see if it matches the description of a funeral bell, deadly webcap, or common conecap. If you can't identify it with full certainty, put it down and walk away!

Another genus that sometimes masquerades as Psilocybe is Hypholoma. Some species of these little brown mushrooms also produce dark purplish spore prints. Hypholoma mushrooms won't kill you, but they won't get you high either. They sometimes cause stomach cramps and vomiting. Hypholoma do not have the gelatinous surface characteristic of a Psilocybe. They typically grow directly from rotting wood, and they appear in dense clumps.

Let's take a look at each of the four most common species of magic mushrooms.

Liberty Caps (Psilocybe semilanceata)

The mushrooms J.S. unwittingly plucked and served to his family that fateful morning were likely liberty caps. One of the most common types of magic mushrooms in the Northern

Hemisphere, liberty caps are easily identifiable by their small, conical cap and yellowish-brown color.

These tiny but powerful mushrooms, also known as pixie caps or witches' hats, are most often found in the colder northern parts of Europe, usually in late summer and fall. They grow in grassy areas like meadows and pastures, particularly those that have been fertilized by cows or sheep. They sometimes grow directly out of dung that has been decomposing for more than one season. More typically, they grow out of the ground after the manure has begun to break down.

Liberty caps have thin stems that can grow up to four inches long. Their bell-shaped caps have a nipple-like protrusion in the center. Most are yellow to brown when young, but they become paler as they age. They have olive-gray gills that turn a dark purple with age. They have a musty odor and are usually found in spring and summer.

Wavy Caps (Psilocybe cyanescens)

Wavy Caps are also common in North America, and they're very similar in appearance to liberty caps. They're easily identifiable by their distinctive wavy caps, which can range in color from white to yellowish brown. These mushrooms grow in wood chips, mulch, and other decaying organic matter.

In the United States, wavy caps are found mainly in the Pacific Northwest where they are a native species. They also grow in the coastal regions of Northern California. Europe, New

Zealand, and Iran are other places they've been spotted. They tend to spread in urban and suburban areas wherever mulch is used to control weeds, so they are increasingly common in parks and manicured yards. You can even spot them in Golden Gate Park!

The diameter of these tiny mushrooms is rarely more than two inches. When mature, the gills are light brown or dark purple and attach broadly to the stipe. A skirt, sometimes gooey with spores, is often left as a remnant of this mushroom's veil on the fibrous, grey or brown stipe.

Flying Saucers (Psilocybe Azurescens)

You will recognize flying saucers by their conical cap and yellowish-brown color. They sometimes grow in dense clusters, and sometimes their pattern is more scattered. These mushrooms grow in sandy, coastal areas, and in the decomposing wood of deciduous trees. They are most abundant in the fall and winter months.

This mushroom was discovered only decades ago near the Columbia River Delta, and its range seems to be limited to the Pacific Northwest.

The cap is bigger than most of the other magic mushrooms species. It can get up to four inches in diameter. It starts out in a conical shape, then flattens with age.

Gold Caps or Cubes (Psilocybe Cubensis)

Gold caps, also called cubes, have larger conical caps that don't flatten out as much. Unlike the other Psilocybe species I've described here, they grow in pastures in more humid and tropical areas, and they are most abundant in the summer months.

The surface of their cap is smooth and sticky. The cap is brown becoming paler at the margin and fades to more of a golden-brown with age. When bruised, all parts of the mushroom stain blue. It has narrow grey gills which darken to purplish-black with age while the gill edges remain whitish. Gold caps have a hollow white stipe.

Magic Mushrooms in Psychotherapy

Psychotherapists have recently started using mushrooms containing psilocybin to help people with depression and other mental health issues, based on the promising results of clinical trials. Psilocybin has also been reported to help people access difficult emotions and explore their inner world in a safe and supported way. Under the direct supervision of trained professionals is the only way I can condone the use of psychedelics, presuming it is legal in your area.

Mushroom foraging is a fun and challenging way to reconnect with the land and can lead to some truly incredible discoveries. If you're looking for a way to reconnect with nature and explore the magical world of psychedelics, mushroom foraging is the perfect activity for you. Just remember to take all the necessary precautions and respect the laws of the area you're in. Psychedelics are not for everyone. If you do decide to forage and sample, proceed with caution!

Not all mushrooms are edible, medicinal, or inclined to give you psychedelic experiences, but that doesn't mean they aren't worth appreciating. There are whole communities of mushroom enthusiasts who go into the forest with cameras instead of baskets, searching for the rare beauties we will discuss in the next chapter.

CHAPTER TEN
The Rare Rubies

Of all the eccentric beings that lurk deep in the forest, mushrooms are some of the most peculiar. They come in the full rainbow of colors, from crimson to violet. Some "bleed" fluids that actually look like blood or rich ink. There are mushrooms that look like furry little animals. Some fungal fruits wave tentacle-like structures that make them look like sea creatures. While most mushrooms use plants as their hosts, a rare few attract insects that they use to spread their spores. And deep in the darkest recesses of the forest, there are mushrooms that glow in the dark.

Bioluminescent Mushrooms

One of the most bizarre features you can find in the mushroom kingdom is bioluminescence. Astonishingly, more than 70 fungal species are capable of producing cold light, thanks to the same combination of oxyluciferin particles, luciferase, and oxygen that allow fireflies to light up their backsides on summer evenings - and in both cases the purpose is the same. While fireflies glow to attract mates, mushrooms shine to allure bugs that will help disperse their spores. In the mushroom world, this phenomenon is known as foxfire.

Most of the mushrooms that glow in the dark grow out of decomposing wood. They appear to follow a 22 to 24-hour cycle that fluctuates based on the ambient temperature, glowing more brightly at night when the humidity is higher, giving them a better chance of dispersing their spores.

By day, bitter oysters (Panellus stipticus) look like a cluster of dull-colored miniature fans attached to decaying wood. At night, their gills and mycelia light up the forest paths like enchanting little lanterns. These are the brightest bioluminescent mushrooms on the planet. The species is very common, but only a few rare strains have developed the ability to light up.

Eternal light mushrooms (Mycena luxaeterna) give off a continuous light, but only from their lime green stipes. They're rarely found outside of the rainforest near Sao Paulo, Brazil.

Bioluminescence requires a lot of energy and other resources. Many of the fungi that have developed this ability limit it to their mycelia, likely as a way to deter animals from eating them. Honey mushrooms, a common edible species in the northern half of the United States, is one example. (Honey mushrooms are edible, but they have poisonous lookalikes that resemble them closely enough that I decided not to include them in this book for beginners.)

Mushrooms that Bleed

You learned about beefsteak fungus, a polypore that bears a striking resemblance to a slab of juicy steak, in Chapter 6. If you're diligent, you may come across other species that produce blood-like or ink-like substances. The bleeding fairy helmet (Mycena haematopus) for one, exudes latex-like red fluid from its burgundy cap when bruised or torn. It's also a bioluminescent mushroom, although its light isn't particularly strong.

Bleeding tooth fungus (Hydnellum peckii) is a rare mushroom that has a particularly macabre appearance. It literally looks like human teeth bleeding from patterned pores. Its pale flesh is dotted with deep pores that seep thick red fluid. Look closely, if you have the stomach for it, and you will see small but nasty looking spines at the base. This mushroom is actually edible, but it reportedly tastes pretty bitter. Some of the chemicals it contains are being tested in treatments for Alzheimer's disease. Keep an eye out for bleeding teeth when you're foraging in the conifer forests of the Pacific Northwest.

Floral Mushrooms

The mushrooms I've selected for this section don't look like mushrooms at all. They are almost perfectly disguised as other objects – usually flowers. One species of mushroom looks, bizarrely, more like a cigar than anything else.

The devil's cigar (Chorioactis geaster) is one that I've got on my bucket list. An extremely rare fungus, it's only been spotted in Texas, Oklahoma, and Japan so far, at roughly the same latitude. When it first pops up, it looks like a cigar standing on end, brown tobacco wrapper and all. When it's ready to release its spores, it splits open into four to six petal-like strips and emits its spores with a hiss and a puff of smoke-like discharge. What's left looks like a woody brown starflower.

Most mushrooms in the marasmius genus look like ordinary agarics, and they are pretty common. Small and lacking in flavor, most species don't get much attention. Marasmius tageticolor is one exception. The dainty cap of this gilled mushroom is creased in a star-like pattern so that it looks like the petals of a violet fused together. What's strikingly different about this mushroom from anything else you'll see is the magenta and white stripes that cover the cap. Tageticolors only grow in Central and South America.

Insectivores

Back in Chapter 4, I revealed to you the interesting tidbit that, unlike humans and animals, fungi digest their food before assimilating it. Most mushroom-producing fungi are vegetarians, but not all. The exceptions look pretty gruesome. Cordyseps are one genus that send spores to infect and kill insects, then transform the insect's remains into a mushroom. Cordyseps are extremely rare in the wild, so scientists are working on methods to cultivate them in labs because they contain a compound that has shown a lot of promise in antiviral and anticancer drugs.

Calling all Citizen Mycologists

There are still a lot of unknowns when it comes to the world of mushrooms. New species are evolving and being discovered all the time. Each year, we learn more about where to find mushrooms that are edible and can be used to treat serious diseases. We're also learning a lot about the crucial role fungi play in their ecosystems.

While you're learning how to forage mushrooms that provide you with savory nutrition, you also have the opportunity to help further scientific understanding. So, keep your eyes open and take note any time you see a mushroom that raises an eyebrow. Your observations could provide valuable information and alert mycologists to important indicators of changes to a mushroom's abundance and distribution. And who knows, you might have a new species of mushroom named after you some day!

CHAPTER ELEVEN
Before You Go Foraging

We've covered a lot of information but before you set out on your first mushroom-hunting expedition, I'm sure you have at least a few more burning questions about exactly how this is done.

- Where will you go?
- What equipment will you need?
- How will you know when you've harvested enough?
- How can you be sure that your mushroom harvest is legal and ethical?

These are all important questions. Personally, I wouldn't venture out into the wild without a thorough answer to each of them. Some of the answers you need are going to be specific to your location, so you will need to do a little bit of research on your own to supplement the information you'll find in this book.

We'll cover the first two of the above questions here in this chapter and save the rest for Chapter Twelve.

Know Where to Go

Understanding your location is one of the basic rules of foraging. You should only ever forage on public lands in areas where you have verified that foraging is allowed. Mushroom hunting on private property is fine as long as you have permission from the property owner. Private forest lands may not look any different from national forests and public parks, but trespassing on private property can get you into a lot of trouble. Rural landowners tend to value their privacy and can be very protective of what's theirs.

Once you've identified a state park, national forest, or private property where you have permission to forage, there's no guarantee that the area is going to be loaded with the kinds of mushrooms you seek. Knowing something about the particular species you're hunting for, along with the plant communities they support, is going to be very helpful in knowing where to look for them. Morels, for example, are never found far from the base of their favorite trees – elm, apple, ash, sycamore, cottonwood, and tulip poplar. (If you find a mushroom that looks like a morel, but it isn't near any of the above trees, don't eat it!)

Some mushrooms flourish in areas that have been recently disturbed while others prefer pristine forest environments. Morels, to use them as an example again, abound in recent burn scars. Say you *are* looking for morels, and you know of a large cottonwood grove where a fire swept through a couple years ago. You might get lucky, and you might not. Hunting for mushrooms, like any other hunting adventure, can be hit or miss. It's a fun challenge, especially if you enjoy spending hours exploring the great outdoors.

Certain areas often yield big harvests year after year, but in most cases, no one is going to tell you where the "good spots" are. Most seasoned mushroom hunters who find good spots don't give up their secrets easily.

Wherever you go looking for your mushrooms, make sure it's a clean environment where the plants look healthy. Stay away from areas with lots of busy traffic and industrial pollution.

Bring What You Need

You will need some basic tools to collect, clean, and transport your forest bounty. This will include:

- A basket, cloth bag, or paper sack
- A second container for mystery mushrooms
- Sheets of aluminum foil for spore prints
- A knife
- A brush
- A garden trowel
- A topographic map
- A permit (where it's required)
- A few good friends
- Your usual hiking gear

Something to Put Them In

A sturdy wicker basket with a handle has been the preferred container for carrying mushrooms ever since people started weaving baskets, and it's probably still your best option. Baskets are relatively easy to carry. They allow the mushrooms to breathe so that they will still be fresh when you get them home. This is also the most forest-friendly option, since it allows the spores that the mushrooms release to fall back down to the forest floor and continue the cycle of life. (Spores are how mushrooms reproduce.)

Paper sacks are convenient, easy to carry, and will allow your mushrooms to breathe. Mesh laundry bags would also work, though I can't imagine anyone collecting a whole laundry bag full of mushrooms. Even if you were lucky enough to find that many and could harvest them ethically, you shouldn't take more than you can use. So, a smaller mesh bag would be good if you have one, or a reusable cotton produce bag.

Small buckets are also used sometimes when harvesting mushrooms that don't bruise too easily. Whatever you do, don't collect mushrooms into plastic bags or they will get slimy, and you won't be able to enjoy them.

A four-frame cartoon that mushrooming enthusiasts like to share online depicts instructions for making a backpack out of a pair of jeans "in an emergency," according to the caption. The third frame shows the jeans filled with morels, and the fourth frame shows the happy mushroom hunter standing naked from the waist down, wearing a denim backpack full of mushrooms.

Made of breathable cotton, a pair of jeans would indeed make a suitable container for mushrooms, but I'm not sure coming upon a patch of morels in the forest without a container would constitute an emergency. The moral of the story is, always bring a suitable container for mushrooms when you go into the forest, even if you're not planning on foraging. That way if you do end up in an unforeseen foraging situation, you won't have to meander around dressed like Donald Duck.

Since you will likely be bringing unknown specimens home to identify later, it's a good idea to bring a second container. That way, any potentially poisonous mushrooms won't be in contact with the ones you're going to eat.

Tools of the Trade

A small knife is an essential tool for mushroom hunting. You will use it to harvest and clean your mushrooms and check them for worms. You can go shopping for a knife that's specifically made for this purpose. Some are even multitools that include little brushes for dusting the mushrooms off before you put them in your basket or sack. That sounds like fun, but your knife really doesn't need to be anything fancy. I always carry a Benchmade folding pocketknife, similar to the knife my dad started me out with when I was twelve.

Here's a pro tip: Wrap some fluorescent tape around your knife hilt so that if you drop it, you'll have a better chance of finding it again. Generally speaking, the forest floor in areas where mushrooms grow tends to be pretty lush.

If your knife doesn't come with a mushroom brush attached, you'll need one of those. You can use a soft-bristle toothbrush or a small paintbrush to clean the soil and loose spores off your mushrooms before bringing them home. Cleaning your mushrooms where you find them is a way of minimizing how much you're taking from the forest (even though we're talking miniscule amounts of biomass here) and it helps give the mushrooms a better chance at making a comeback next year.

A garden trowel isn't always necessary, but it's a fine idea to carry one in case you need to dig up an entire mushroom so you can identify it. Picking or cutting mushrooms is usually recommended to give the mycelia (the whole organism that the mushrooms we see and eat are only a small part of) a chance to fruit next year. So don't use your trowel unless you have no other way to figure out what kind of mushroom you're dealing with.

On many public lands, digging into the ground is illegal. If you're foraging in an area where digging is legal and pulling up the entire mushroom is the only way to identify it, make sure you're disturbing the ground as little as possible. When you're done, cover the ground with ample forest litter so the mycelia you leave behind won't dry out.

Don't forget to bring sheets of aluminum foil so you can take spore prints while your mushrooms are fresh. Simply cut off the stems and wrap the caps in foil as soon as you harvest the mushroom in question, and continue foraging.

The Paperwork

In some locations, a permit is required to harvest mushrooms. Always check with the appropriate governing authorities, and make sure you're aware of all of the regulations surrounding where you can harvest mushrooms, what methods are allowed, and how much you are allowed to take.

I recommend either carrying a topographic map or a mobile device that can tell you your elevation when you're foraging in rough terrain. Not only will this help you keep from getting lost, but it will also help you locate specimens that only grow at certain elevations.

As far as getting lost, you may not think you have much to worry about, but even experienced mushroom hunters foraging in familiar terrain lose their bearings every year. It's easy to lose track of your whereabouts when your attention is focused on the ground.

Your Crew

Foraging for mushrooms in a group is a good idea for a couple of different reasons, especially when you're just starting out. One of the fun things that I love about mushroom hunting is that there's so much to learn. Mushrooms are mysterious organisms that we humans still don't know much about. You're bound to have questions that one of your buddies may be able to answer. Another reason to bring friends is that the more eyes scanning the forest floor, the more mushrooms you're likely to find. And finally, as in any wilderness situation, there's safety in numbers. Just be careful not to bring too much foot traffic into one area.

I often see families with small children combing the forests for morels in the spring, just after a good rain. It always warms my heart to see kids learning wilderness survival skills early in life, but I've found that the parents often have an ulterior motive for bringing their offspring on these seasonal treasure hunts. Morels come in brown and dull yellow-orange shades that are notoriously hard to pick out from the background of decaying leaves and logs on the forest floor. The sharp eyes of children are often more successful than those of their parents and grandparents.

Standard Hiking Gear

Foraging for mushrooms makes for hours of fun. You will be amazed at how the time flies! When preparing for your first mushrooming expedition, keep in mind that you will be doing a lot of hiking as you explore new terrain, and you will want to be prepared to enjoy your forest adventure safely and comfortably. Bring snacks and water. Wear good shoes, brightly colored clothing, and dress for the weather.

CHAPTER TWELVE
The Spotless Forager

Mushroom hunting is a great way to immerse yourself in the natural world, add nutrient-dense snacks to your diet, and practice self-preservation skills in the wild. This fascinating hobby, which has become wildly popular from coast to coast in recent years, is not without risks. Before you go mushrooming, you will want to become familiar with health risks, legal restrictions, and the ways your foraging forays can impact the web of life that all of us, including the mushrooms, depend on.

With a little bit of care and effort, you can put into practice a few guidelines to ensure that you have a great time, go home with a delicious bounty, and leave the forest environment intact for future foragers. Here are some basic rules of safety and etiquette to help you determine which mushrooms to pick and which ones to leave behind:

- Don't pick it unless you're going to eat it.
- Don't pick it if you're not sure it's safe.
- Don't pick it if it's rare – leave it for others to admire!

Personal Safety

Thousands of different types of mushrooms grow in the forests of North America, and many of the edible varieties closely resemble their poisonous relatives. This is why a staggering 7,000+ cases of mushroom poisoning are reported each year in the United States. Of those 7,000, up to 40 result in long-term harm. Three mushroom poisonings each year prove to be fatal. (Brandenburg & Ward, 2018.)

Even if an experimental nibble doesn't kill you, the effects of mushroom poisoning can be pretty uncomfortable and downright scary, especially if you're deep in the wilderness and can't easily access medical attention.

So, as an important rule of thumb, don't put anything in your mouth unless you're absolutely certain of what it is and how it will affect you. If you don't have a mushroom expert to guide you on your first few hunts, you will likely be collecting only one or two samples of each specimen and bringing them home for proper identification before you go back into the forest and fill your basket.

Use all of your senses when you're trying to determine whether a mushroom is edible or poisonous. Guidebooks, mushroom identification apps, and websites can be helpful. A good guidebook will describe not only what a mushroom looks like but also things like its texture, how it smells, how dense it feels in your hand, what happens when it bruises, and how it develops and ages throughout its lifecycle. If you're having a hard time narrowing a mushroom down between multiple similar species, consult at least two sources that have detailed information and close-up photos before deciding that your specimen is safe to eat.

Identifying mushrooms can take time. In some cases, part of the process is making a spore print by blotting the gills onto a piece of paper, then letting it sit overnight.

When to Pick It and When to Leave it Alone

Once you've identified your specimen and started looking around for more of them, it can be easy to get caught up in the fun and pick more than you can use. If you pick an area too clean, there won't be much left for the next group of mushroom foragers that comes through. This is why I recommend making a plan for how you're going to prepare and/or preserve your mushrooms before you set out on your foraging adventure. Some kinds of mushrooms need to be cooked and eaten right away, while others can be dried or frozen and kept for months. Another thing to keep in mind is allergies. Make sure you're not allergic to the mushrooms you plan to pick so that they don't go to waste.

And no, in most cases you can't sell the surplus. Selling mushrooms that you harvest on public lands is almost always a no-no that can result in hefty fines, if not jail time. Many of the National Forests in Washington State, where I encountered the two grandmothers that I described in the introduction to this book, are an exception. These Forests offer "Commercial Use" permits that will, for a price, allow you to collect up to 120 gallons of mushrooms that you are allowed to turn around and sell. I don't know whether the two grandmothers I encountered on the Olympic Peninsula had purchased such a permit, and I don't consider it any of my business.

Selling mushrooms that you've harvested on your own private property or with permission from the property owner is fine, of course, as long as you've properly identified the mushrooms you're selling, and you're sure they're safe to eat.

Low-Impact Foraging

It may surprise you to learn that the mushroom patches that occur in nature are remarkably resilient so overharvesting isn't much of an issue for most species. This is because the mushrooms we pick and eat aren't the whole plant. They're just the fruit, or "fruiting body" if you want to get technical. Think of it like picking an apple tree clean of apples – it doesn't harm the tree at all. Unless a mushroom's supporting mycelial network is damaged, mushrooms will fruit in exactly the same places year after year.

There is some debate among the mushrooming community over whether it's better to cut mushrooms with a knife or pick them. Some foragers prefer to slice mushrooms neatly from the forest floor while others pluck them with their hands, mimicking the way bears, rabbits, squirrels, and wild boars pluck mushrooms with their teeth and paws. They worry that cutting with a knife could leave the mycelia more vulnerable to pathogens. This matter has actually been studied by scientists, and they've found that neither method seems to be better or worse than the other (Norvell & Roger, 2016).

What's more of an issue than overharvesting is when the plants that mushrooms depend on get trampled and when litter is left behind in the forest, sadly a common occurrence in many of the most popular mushroom hunting grounds. So, work your mushroom patches in small groups and tread lightly. If you come to an area that looks like it's been getting a lot of foot traffic, give it a break and let it recover for a while. And of course, practice the golden rule of pack-it-in pack-it-out.

Laws and Regulations

Mushroom foraging may seem pretty straightforward. Find the mushroom, identify the mushroom, verify that it's edible, cook the mushroom, and eat the mushroom. Right? But it's important to know that there are serious laws and regulations that must be followed. Pick the wrong mushroom in the wrong location, and you could be looking at hefty fines or even jail time! In the US, each state has its own rules surrounding the collection of wild mushrooms, and you will want to get familiar with the ones that pertain to your area before embarking on your mushroom-hunting adventure. In addition to state laws, individual parks, park systems, and other bodies that govern public lands have their own restrictions and guidelines.

Most states require a permit in order to forage for mushrooms, but the rules and regulations vary from state to state. In California, where I live, mushroom hunting is only allowed in one public area – Salt Point State Park. Located just under 100 miles up the coast from San Francisco, this 6,000-acre park offers 20 miles of gorgeous hiking trails, many of which overlook the Pacific Ocean. People come from all over the state to enjoy this park for a wide variety of activities, one of which is foraging for mushrooms.

Forage anywhere in California without a permit, even if you're on private property, and you're flirting with a penalty of up to $1000 and up to six months in jail. As much as I love the topography of my home state, it's draconian penalties like this that make me certain I must eventually relocate to a place where I can more freely exercise my love of nature.

In Oregon, foraging for mushrooms is not permitted in state parks, but is allowed on some other public lands.

Some states, like Pennsylvania, do not require a permit for foraging for mushrooms, but it is still important to check with the local authorities or park rangers before you begin combing the forests for those savory little morsels.

In addition to the basic rules about whether or not mushroom foraging is allowed, many states, parks, and other public areas have restrictions on the types of mushrooms you can collect, methods you're allowed to use, the amounts that you're allowed to take home, and whether you're allowed to sell them after you remove them from the forest, so be sure to get familiar with the rules and guidelines for each site you visit.

Past generations were allowed to forage far and wide with few restrictions to worry about. Most foragers were practicing family traditions that went back centuries, and they knew very well how to collect mushrooms in a way that minimized harm and risk. Any minor infractions were a rare occurrence and were most often ignored.

Things have changed over the last few years as mushrooming has become a popular hobby among the younger generation. Personally, I'm glad to see that so many young people are serious about self-sufficiency and are taking the time to learn wilderness survival skills. Not to be a doomer, but I don't expect our local supermarkets to be stocked to their ceilings with every mycelial delight you can imagine indefinitely. There may very well come a time when knowing how to forage for mushrooms and other plants could save your life. It's reassuring to see kids these days at least getting a taste for the self-reliant lifestyle.

With more and more people venturing into the forests to seek its meaty little treasures, it's unsurprising that new laws have sprung up as a response. Laws around mushroom foraging are intended to:

- Protect foragers from inadvertently poisoning themselves
- Ensure that there are enough mushrooms left in the forests for critters that depend on them
- Protect the ecosystems of which mushrooms are an integral part.

Ecologists worry that mushroom hunters and other foragers, who flock to the park because there's nowhere else in the state to go, are causing excessive damage to the environment. Mushroom hunters and other foragers wander off established trails and make new trails, trampling delicate plants and distributing plant pathogens that they unknowingly carry in from other locales.

My view is that if mushroom foraging were legal in more areas throughout the state, as it was in the not-too-distant past, the burden on Salt Point State Park would be eased. It's possible that other parks would benefit as well, as they would see more visitors who understand the value of a living, functioning ecosystem and will take care to preserve it. Most foraging enthusiasts understand that if we want to continue to enjoy wild mushrooms and other plants for years and generations to come, we must do our part to maintain the ecosystems where they thrive.

In the past, foraging laws didn't often have sharp teeth. These days, foraging in a place where you're not allowed, collecting the wrong species, or foraging over your limit could result in up to six months in jail! So, it's worth doing some research to find out what the local regulations are before you start collecting mushrooms from your nearby forests. I don't know about you, but I can't go back to jail. Just kidding! They probably miss me.

Go directly to the source (government offices and websites) instead of relying on second-hand information about what's allowed and what's forbidden in the world of mushroom foraging. In some places, especially where regulations have recently changed or if they differ from park to park within a small area, there is a lot of confusion surrounding where foraging for mushrooms is allowed, what species can be harvested, how much you're allowed to take, and what methods are approved. Don't be discouraged if the laws seem vague or are hard to track down. Keep asking until you get clear answers.

While it might be tempting to casually pick a mushroom or two in an area where you haven't gone through the process of getting a permit, I do not recommend it! There can be serious consequences. In most places where it's prohibited, it's considered a misdemeanor – an actual crime!

Aside from keeping you out of jail or protecting your wallet from fines, going and getting a permit is actually an opportunity to learn more about the area where you will be foraging, especially if you do it in person. Ask the park ranger, or whoever is serving you any questions you have about personal safety in that particular area, things you need to know to manage your ecological footprint, and any poisonous mushrooms in the area that you will want to be sure to avoid.

Do you have any specific areas in mind where you would like to start foraging? In the next and final chapter, I'll introduce you to some of the best locales for mushroom hunting in the United States.

CHAPTER THIRTEEN
Forward, Forager!

Whether you're searching for mushrooms to eat, use for medicinal purposes, or just to observe, there are a wealth of locations and opportunities all across the United States. You've already learned a lot in this book, but we have a little more ground to cover before you're ready to grab your basket and get started.

Do you know the best places to forage? What are the foraging rules of your area? Find out the answers to these questions and more know-before-you-go tidbits in this chapter. I'll give you some tips on how to have a successful hunt in each of the eight regions of the continental United States: Pacific Northwest, North Central, Midwest, Northeast, Southeast, South Central, Southwest, and Alaska. I'll point out the most common edibles and the poisonous mushrooms you're most likely to come across in each region.

The best places to forage for wild edible mushrooms in the US

Now that we've discussed regulations surrounding mushroom hunting and the consequences of disregarding them, let's take a look at several places you can go to have an incredible mushroom foraging experience that, with any luck, will result in a delicious dinner or two.

Pacific Northwest

The Pacific Northwest is a great area for mushrooming. There are thousands of acres of public forests that are full of the dark, moist, tree-filled environments where mushrooms proliferate. If you're lucky enough to live in this area, you should be able to find a local group of mycophiles who go on mushrooming expeditions together. There are also fungi festivals and other events where you can celebrate mushrooms, learn more about them, and connect with others who share this fun and fascinating hobby.

Some of the best places I've found in the Northwest for harvesting wild edible mushrooms include Olympic National Park, Mount Rainier National Park, and Mount St. Helens National Volcanic Monument. These parks are home to a variety of tasty fungi including chanterelles, morels, porcini, and many others. You can often find multiple species growing within easy walking distance of each other in the fall, so you will get to sample a variety, whether you visit in the spring, summer, or fall. Watch out for the funeral bell (Galerina marginata), a deadly variety that calls this region home.

On the Oregon Coast and in the Coast Range, as well as the Cascade Mountains, you can find a variety of mushrooms. Northern California is also a great place to explore while looking for mushrooms, with its mild winters and stunning variety of ecosystems.

Olympic National Park is one of the best places to find wild edible mushrooms in the Pacific Northwest, and it's home to a smorgasbord of wild edible plants as well. The park harbors at least 1400 different species of fungi and accounts for at least 56% of Washington State's mushroom diversity. The peak season is after the start of fall rains, and it continues up until the first major frost. You can legally collect one quart per person, per day. The most popular areas for mushroom hunting within the park are near the Quinault, Lake Cushman, and Sol Duc Valley areas of the Olympic Peninsula. Mount Rainier National Park in Washington is another great spot for mushroom foraging.

North Central

The North Central states offer plenty of foraging opportunities. You can find chanterelles, chicken of the woods, lion's mane, maitake, morels, oyster, and reishi mushrooms.

If you're in the area, be sure to visit the Village of Weyerhaeuser in Wisconsin. Mushroom hunting is a beloved pastime among the locals. The surrounding area features a broad range of mushrooms, but it's most well-known for its morels.

Watch out for the destroying angel (Amanita virosa) when foraging in this region. Found in wooded areas, such as parks and forests, this beauty can be fatal if eaten in large enough quantities.

Midwest

The Midwest offers a variety of great places to forage for mushrooms. From the rolling hills of southern Wisconsin to the Ozarks in Iowa and Missouri, and from the forested areas of the northern states, to the Loess Hills and Missouri River Valley, delectable mushrooms are everywhere. Michigan's Upper Peninsula and the humid alpine forests of the Appalachian Mountains are especially fruitful grounds for mushroom hunting.

Mark Twain National Forest is a favorite spot of mine, with its rolling hills and lush vegetation. I always have an incredible time. There are dozens of unique species to find.

The most common poisonous mushroom in this region is the false parasol (Chlorophyllum molybdites). A large mushroom with white cap and gills, it is found in lawns, gardens, and wooded areas. It can be mistaken for the common button mushroom, which is much smaller.

Northeast

When I'm visiting the North Atlantic states, I like to go mushrooming in the Adirondack Mountains in New York, the White Mountains in New Hampshire, and the Green Mountains in Vermont. Each of these ranges is home to a variety of wild edibles including morels, puffballs, and boletes. The best time to plan your trip is late spring or early summer.

Acadia National Park has become increasingly popular in recent years for its range of mushroom species including two of everyone's favorites – chanterelles and morels. If you go, be sure to stay on the established trails. Some areas are closed to mushroom picking, so study your map carefully and watch for signs along the trails to make sure you haven't wandered out of the areas where you're allowed to forage.

False morels are common in the grassy areas of this region. They won't kill you, but they will make you pretty uncomfortable.

Southeast

Some of the best places to forage for mushrooms in the South are the Cherokee National Forest in Tennessee, the Great Smoky Mountains National Park in Tennessee and North Carolina, and the Ocala National Forest in Florida. Here you will find chanterelles, morels, and boletes. Spring, early summer, and late fall are the best seasons for foraging.

There are some great spots along the Appalachian Trail where the forests are dense. Hot Springs, North Carolina in particular is a great spot for chanterelles, chicken of the woods, lion's mane, maitake, morels, oyster mushrooms, and reishi mushrooms.

Destroying angels (Amanita virosa), false morels (Clitocybe Rivulosa), jack o' lantern mushrooms (Omphalotus illudens), and death caps (Amanita phalloides) all grow in this region.

South Central

The South Central states including Texas, Arkansas, Oklahoma, and New Mexico and Louisiana offer plenty of great places to forage for mushrooms. In Arkansas, the Ozarks and the Ouachita Mountains are particularly prolific. You can also find plenty of mushrooms in the wooded areas of Oklahoma. There are mushrooms to forage in the hill country of Texas, Big

Bend National Park, and the Piney Woods. Additionally, in Louisiana, you can find mushrooms in the swamps and bayous of the state.

Walnut Creek in Davy Crockett National Forest in eastern Texas is a popular spot. This area is known for its abundance of chanterelles. Oysters, morel, and other edible mushrooms can also be found in the forest.

Destroying angels are common here as well.

Southwest

In my own stomping grounds, you can find morels, chanterelles, and porcini in the Grand Canyon and in Saguaro National Park in Arizona.

Salt Point State Park, located in the rugged northern part of Sonoma County, is one of the few places in California where mushroom picking is allowed. The park is home to a variety of edible mushrooms including candy caps, russula, boletes, witch's butter, chanterelles, and many others. The park imposes a bag limit of three pounds per day, so be sure to stay within that limit.

The most common poisonous mushroom in the Southwest is the death cap (Amanita phalloides), a mushroom that leads to death in over half of the cases where it is consumed.

Alaska

Alaska is home to a variety of wild edible mushrooms, including morels, chanterelles, and porcini. Tongass National Forest is legendary among mushroom enthusiasts, as are Chugach National Forest and Denali National Park and Preserve.

Tongass National Forest is the largest national forest in the United States, covering most of Southeast Alaska. It boasts several species of edible mushrooms including the king bolete, fire morels, and pacific golden chanterelles. Chugach National Forest, in Southcentral Alaska, is also home to many edible mushroom species. Both forests offer great opportunities for mushroom hunters, although most mushroom enthusiasts agree that Tongass is the more productive area.

Beware of the funeral bell (Galerina Marginata), also known as the deadly galerina.

Frequently Asked Questions about Mushroom Hunting

Mushroom foraging can be a daunting activity, after all, if you don't know exactly what you're doing, you could end up in the emergency room or worse. You now know more than most beginners about where and how to find the most delicious forest edibles, and you should be ready to venture into the forest, basket in hand, with confidence. In case you still have any questions, though, I've put together some answers to the ones that I hear most often.

Q: What should I do if I get lost?

A: Getting lost while foraging for mushrooms is surprisingly easy to do. Your eyes are on the ground, focused on small details as you go from tree trunk to tree trunk, peering under logs and leaves until you suddenly realize you're not anywhere near the trail and your mushrooming companions are out of earshot.

If this happens, don't panic. Don't start wandering in an attempt to find your way back – that's a good way to get even more lost. Check your map or compass to see if you can get your bearings. You should also have a phone or a whistle you can blow if you're out of cell phone range. If you don't have either of those, look for landmarks such as streams, rivers, or mountain ranges that you can use as a point of reference as you slowly move through the area looking for more clues as to where you are. Note the position of the sun in the sky, as that will help you get a sense of direction. The sun will be generally southeast of you before noon, and it will be southwest of you in the afternoon. As a rule of thumb, make your way toward open areas or clearings, and always move downhill if you're on a mountain or rough terrain.

If you're ever planning on going into the forest alone, make sure someone knows where you are going and when you plan on coming back. Bring plenty of snacks and water in case it does take longer to get back than you anticipate.

Q: What about ticks?

A: Encountering ticks is an unfortunate possibility when foraging in most forested lands. Lyme disease is an increasingly common tick-borne illness that infects over 300,000 people each year in the United States. While cases have been reported in all 50 states, it's most common in the Northeast and Midwest.

Fortunately, there are several things you can do to protect yourself from ticks and the diseases they carry if you plan on foraging in a heavily tick-infested area. First, wear insect repellent that contains picaridin, oil of lemon eucalyptus (OLE), or PMD. Second, spray your clothing, gear, and hiking footwear with permethrin, an insecticide that kills mosquitos, black flies, and ticks. Inspect yourself at least once a day and check the hotspots on your body that ticks gravitate toward.

Q: Can I drink out of streams and creeks?

A: I would strongly advise against drinking directly from any forest stream. Although streams usually look pristine, they are often contaminated with bacteria, parasites, and other contaminants. If you plan to drink from a stream, it's best to purify, boil, or filter the water first to ensure it's safe.

Before you go, I've prepared a checklist of items that you are likely to either need or want. These items will help you ensure that your foraging adventures are safe, fruitful and fun.

Mushroom Foraging Checklist

Item	Needed Y/N	Packed Y/N
Basket or bag for edibles		
Basket or bag for questionables		
Foil for spore prints		
Knife for harvesting, cleaning & trimming		
Garden trowel		
Permit		
Compass		
Map		
Whistle		
Insect repellent		
Water		
Water filter		
Snacks		

I hope this guide has provided you with all the information you need to embark on your wild mushroom foraging adventure. Whatever corner of the country you're in, there are a variety of places to explore and delicious mushrooms to find. But remember, it is always important to obtain a permit before foraging for mushrooms and to be familiar with the different types of mushrooms in your area before harvesting them.

That's it! You have made it this far, and now it's time to go even further… get out in the wild today and start foraging!

Sharing Your Bounty

As you start implementing everything you've learned and your foraging expeditions bring home greater bounties, it's natural that you'll want to spread the word.

Simply by leaving your honest opinion of this book on Amazon, you'll show new readers where they can find all the guidance they need to experience the joys of foraging too – and do so safely.

LEAVE A REVIEW!

Foraging is such an enriching experience… and doing it safely is crucial. Thank you for helping me share the guidance new foragers need to do exactly that.

CONCLUSION

Congratulations, intrepid forager of fungi! With the knowledge you've gained in this this book, you are now ready to embark on your journey into the wild. I'm excited to think about all that you will discover in the wonderful world of mushrooms as you venture into the forest.

You are about to see for yourself the fascinating relationship between mushrooms and the rest of the beings in the forest. Equipped with a new understanding of the importance of foraging sustainably, you now know how to identify the most common edible mushrooms, you're familiar with the most common and the most deadly poisonous varieties to avoid, and you even know a little bit about some of the mushrooms that can keep you well and treat injuries and illnesses. You've been introduced to psychoactive mushrooms, and you've learned about a selection of bizarre and beautiful mushrooms that are just amazing to look at.

With an open mind and a sense of adventure, I hope that you continue to learn and explore the world of mushrooms. This is just the beginning, after all, and there's a lot more to know!

In this book, we've covered basic safety tips for foraging in the wild. Always remember that when you are out in nature, you are at the mercy of the elements. It is up to you to protect yourself and the environment by following a few simple rules.

- Check the weather
- Know your surroundings
- Bring the proper equipment
- Forage in good company
- Be prepared for emergencies
- Stay on trails
- Don't eat anything unless you're absolutely certain it's edible

Now that you know how to recognize some of the most abundant and delicious species of edible mushrooms, you can be more self-reliant and less dependent on a food system that is increasingly unreliable and expensive. I will never forget the first meal I prepared using mushrooms that I foraged myself. It will give you so much peace of mind to know that you will never have to go hungry as long as you're surrounded by nature.

For more ways to learn about mushrooms and deepen your appreciation for them:

- Join our Facebook group: Consummate Survivors Community
- Join a foraging club
- Attend mushroom lectures, workshops, and other events in your area
- Read more books on mycology
- Visit a mycology exhibit at your nearest museum of natural history

Fungi are one of the most important and least understood organisms on the planet. They are essential to regulating the health of forest ecosystems, and they play a significant role in human health and wellbeing. Yet fungi are often overlooked, misunderstood, and underappreciated. Because of their importance, it is essential that we learn more about the fungi around us and in us.

Mushrooms are so much more than pizza toppings. There is so much readily available information to learn about them, and even more that is yet to be discovered. It's time to unearth it all! As a budding citizen mycologist, what will you discover on your next (or first?) foray into the forest?

If your interest in foraging goes beyond just mushrooms, I would encourage you to pick up a copy of my first book "Master the World of Edible Wild Plants", in which I discus dozens of non-mushroom plants and their foraging practices. Don't forget to post a review of this book on Amazon to let others know how much you learned from this book! Your positive words can help others find a new path toward sustainability and help offset the negativity that is all too common in the online world. Also, if you'd like to become part of a welcoming and informative community of active survivalists, you can join our Facebook group, the Consummate Survivors Community; https://www.facebook.com/groups/6058492810897339

Happy foraging and Semper Fidelis

BIBLIOGRAPHY

"4 Tips for Choosing the Best Mushroom Supplements | Gaia Herbs®: Gaia Herbs®." Gaia Herbs, https://www.gaiaherbs.com/blogs/seeds-of-knowledge/4-tips-for-choosing-high-quality-mushroom-supplements-to-support-your-health#:~:text=Tip%20%231%3A%20Choose%20Products%20Made,you%20the%20strongest%20wellness%20support.

"6 Ways Mushrooms Can Help Save the Planet." Hub for Circular Economy, https://crclr.org/article/2017-05-01-6-ways-mushrooms-can-help-save-the-planet.

"7 Mushroom Health Benefits - Eating Mushrooms Side Effects." Good Housekeeping, Good Housekeeping, 3 June 2019, https://www.goodhousekeeping.com/health/diet-nutrition/a27633487/mushroom-health-benefits/.

"7 of the World's Most Poisonous Mushrooms." Encyclopædia Britannica, Encyclopædia Britannica, https://www.britannica.com/list/7-of-the-worlds-most-poisonous-mushrooms.

"8 Best Places to Go Foraging in the US in 2022 - Lonely Planet." Lonely Planet, https://facebook.com/lonelyplanet, https://www.lonelyplanet.com/articles/best-us-foraging-spots.

"11 Edible Mushrooms in the US (And How to Tell They're Not Toxic)." Plantsnap - Identify Plants, Trees, Mushrooms With An App, https://www.facebook.com/PlantSnap/, 4 Dec. 2018, https://www.plantsnap.com/blog/edible-mushrooms-united-states/.

"A Complete History of Mushrooms - Drug Rehab Options." Drug Rehab Options, https://www.facebook.com/AmericanAddictionCenters, 26 Mar. 2013, https://rehabs.com/blog/a-complete-history-of-mushrooms/.

"A Guide to All the Different Types of Psychedelic Mushrooms." MEL Magazine, https://www.facebook.com/melmagazine/, 21 Apr. 2022, https://melmagazine.com/en-us/story/types-of-psychedelic-mushrooms.

"A Magical World Of Rare Mushrooms Revealed By Steve Axford | DeMilked." Demilked, https://www.facebook.com/demilked/, 20 May 2014, https://www.demilked.com/fungi-mushroom-photography-steve-axford/.

Adams, Dwight. "Morel Mushroom Season Has Arrived. Here's What You Need to Know." The Indianapolis Star, IndyStar, 3 Apr. 2018, https://www.indystar.com/story/news/2018/04/03/morel-mushrooms-heres-what-you-need-know/483541002/.

"Apricot Jelly Identification: Pictures, Habitat, Season & Spore Print | Guepinia Helvelloides." Edible Wild Food, Recipes | Weeds, Fungi, Flowers & Foraging, https://www.ediblewildfood.com/apricot-jelly.aspx.

Apse, Will. "Types of Fungi: Mushrooms, Toadstools, Molds, and More - Owlcation." Owlcation, Owlcation, 11 Sept. 2011, https://owlcation.com/stem/types_of_fungi.

Auteri, Monica. "Finding Porcini Mushrooms: Useful Advice | Italian Traditions." Italian Traditions, 5 Oct. 2017, https://italian-traditions.com/finding-porcini-mushrooms-useful-advice/.

"Benefits of Fungi for the Environment and Humans." UN Decade on Restoration, https://www.decadeonrestoration.org/stories/benefits-fungi-environment-and-humans.

"Boletus Edulis, Cep, Penny Bun Bolete Mushroom." Wildflowers, Wild Orchids, Fungi, Wildlife; Nature Books, Reserves, https://www.first-nature.com/fungi/boletus-edulis.php.

Bradley, Kirsten. "Foraging + Using Turkeytail Mushrooms - Trametes Versicolour - Milkwood: Permaculture Courses, Skills + Stories." Milkwood: Permaculture Courses, Skills + Stories, https://www.facebook.com/Milkwood, 13 Aug. 2017, https://www.milkwood.net/2017/08/14/foraging-using-turkeytail-mushrooms-trametes-versicolour/.

"Candy Cap Mushrooms Information, Recipes and Facts." Specialty Produce Is San Diego's Best Wholesale Distributor, https://specialtyproduce.com/produce/Candy_Cap_Mushrooms_9803.php.

Cooke, Justin. "List of Psilocybin Mushroom Species (And Other Psychoactive Fungi) - Tripsitter." Tripsitter, 12 Sept. 2021, https://tripsitter.com/magic-mushrooms/species/.

"Debunking the World's Largest Mushroom Photo." Waffles at Noon. (2016). https://wafflesatnoon.com/debunking-the-worlds-largest-mushroom-photo

DiBenedetto, Chase. "A Beginner's Guide To Urban Foraging - Social Good." Mashable India, Mashable India, 13 Nov. 2020, https://in.mashable.com/social-good/18273/a-beginners-guide-to-urban-foraging.

Dy, Kiki. "A Brief History of Magic Mushrooms Across Ancient Civilizations | Psychedelic Spotlight." Psychedelic Spotlight, 11 Aug. 2021, https://psychedelicspotlight.com/history-of-magic-mushrooms-across-ancient-civilizations/.

"Economic Importance of Mushroom | Agriculture." Essays, Research Papers and Articles on Agriculture in India, 21 Apr. 2018, https://www.agricultureinindia.net/vegetables-2/mushroom-vegetables-2/economic-importance-of-mushroom-agriculture/18084.

"Exploring the Role of Mushrooms Throughout History - Minnesota – R&R Cultivation." R&R Cultivation, https://rrcultivation.com/blogs/mn/exploring-the-role-of-mushrooms-throughout-history.

Ferment, Grow Forage Cook. "6 Medicinal Mushrooms for Your Health." Grow Forage Cook Ferment, 1 Feb. 2019, https://www.growforagecookferment.com/medicinal-mushrooms/.

"Foraging for Beginners: Tips for Safely Gathering Wild, Edible Foods | GORE-TEX Brand." Waterproof, Windproof & Breathable Clothing | GORE-TEX Brand, https://www.gore-tex.com/blog/foraging-food-wild-plants.

"Foraging For Berries and Feeding the Homeless Shouldn't Be Crimes - Reason Foundation." Reason Foundation, https://www.facebook.com/ReasonFoundation/, 20 July 2021, https://reason.org/commentary/foraging-for-berries-and-feeding-the-homeless-shouldnt-be-crimes/.

"Foraging For Wild Medicinal Mushrooms | Garden Culture Magazine." Garden Culture Magazine, https://facebook.com/gardenculture, 5 July 2021, https://gardenculturemagazine.com/foraging-for-wild-medicinal-mushrooms/.

"Foraging Legality — Four Season Foraging." Four Season Foraging, Four Season Foraging, 1 Apr. 2019, https://www.fourseasonforaging.com/blog/2019/3/19/foraging-legality.

"Foraging Rules & Regulations on Public Land - Feral Foraging." Feral Foraging - Return to the Wild, https://facebook.com/feralforaging, 17 June 2020, https://feralforaging.com/foraging-rules-and-regulations/.

"Fungi: Poisonous Mushroom Look Alikes." Mushroom Exam - Online Mushroom Identification Training, https://mushroomexam.com/mushroom_look_alikes.html.

"Guide to Medicinal Mushrooms: Types, Best Uses and Recipes." Academy of Culinary Nutrition, 13 Feb. 2019, https://www.culinarynutrition.com/guide-to-medicinal-mushrooms-types-best-uses-and-recipes/.

"Hallucinogenic Mushrooms Drug Profile | Www.Emcdda.Europa.Eu." EMCDDA Home Page | Www.Emcdda.Europa.Eu, https://www.emcdda.europa.eu/publications/drug-profiles/hallucinogenic-mushrooms_en.

Harrell, Ashley. "'The Mad Mushroom Rush': As a Popular Hobby Has Exploded, It's Straining Salt Point State Park." SFGATE, SFGATE, 6 Dec. 2021, https://www.sfgate.com/california-parks/article/California-mushroom-rush-salt-point-state-park-16672299.php.

Healy, Paula. "Mushrooms: Vital to Ecosystems - Smithsonian Gardens." Smithsonian Gardens, https://www.facebook.com/SmithsonianGardens, 8 Sept. 2020, https://gardens.si.edu/learn/blog/mushrooms-vital-to-ecosystems-and-a-culinary-delight/.

Heimbuch, Jaymi. "13 Bizarre and Beautiful Mushrooms." Treehugger, Treehugger, 7 Aug. 2013, https://www.treehugger.com/most-bizarre-mushrooms-4858744.

Hitt, Caitlyn. "History of Magic Mushrooms: When Were Psilocybin Mushrooms Discovered? - Thrillist." Thrillist, Thrillist, 26 Aug. 2020, https://www.thrillist.com/news/nation/history-of-magic-mushrooms-origin-story-facts.

"How to Forage Wild Oyster Mushrooms — Book Wild Food Foraging Classes Online | ForageSF." Book Wild Food Foraging Classes Online | ForageSF, Book Wild Food Foraging Classes Online | ForageSF, 5 Mar. 2019, https://www.foragesf.com/blog/2019/3/5/how-to-forage-wild-oyster-mushrooms.

"Identifying Mushrooms: There Is More to It than You Might Realize - MSU Extension." MSU Extension, 9 Sept. 2016, https://www.canr.msu.edu/news/identifying_mushrooms_there_is_more_to_it_than_you_might_realize.

Janikian, Michelle. "Psilocybe Cubensis and Other Types of Magic Mushrooms You Should Know - DoubleBlind Mag." DoubleBlind Mag, https://www.facebook.com/doubleblindmag/, https://doubleblindmag.com/mushrooms/types/psilocybe-cubensis-magic-mushrooms/.

Keough, Ben. "Here's What You'll Need to Start Foraging Mushrooms | Wirecutter." Wirecutter: Reviews for the Real World, The New York Times, https://www.nytimes.com/wirecutter/blog/how-to-hunt-mushrooms/.

Kostelny, Laura. "12 Different Types of Mushrooms - Most Common Kinds of Edible Mushrooms." Country Living, Country Living, 3 Dec. 2019, https://www.countryliving.com/food-drinks/g29993727/types-of-mushrooms/.

La Forge, Tiffany. "6 Mushrooms That Act as Turbo-Shots for Your Immune System." Healthline, Healthline Media, 5 Apr. 2018, https://www.healthline.com/health/food-nutrition/best-medicinal-mushrooms-to-try.

MediaWize. "George Seryogin on How to Legally Hunt Wild Mushrooms | OCNJ Daily." OCNJ Daily, OCNJ Daily, 28 Oct. 2021, https://ocnjdaily.com/george-seryogin-legally-hunt-wild-mushrooms/.

"Meet the Mushrooms - Different Types of Fungi | Mushroom Mountain." Mushroom Mountain, https://mushroommountain.com/meet-the-mushrooms/.

Mulcahy, Lisa. "7 Mushroom Health Benefits - Eating Mushrooms Side Effects." Good Housekeeping, Good Housekeeping, 3 June 2019, https://www.goodhousekeeping.com/health/diet-nutrition/a27633487/mushroom-health-benefits/.

"Mushroom Checklist | What to Look for When Buying Medicinal Mushrooms | Inner Atlas." Inner Atlas , https://www.facebook.com/inneratlasAU, 22 Mar. 2021, https://www.inneratlas.com.au/blogs/journal/checklist-what-to-look-for-when-buying-medicinal-mushrooms.

"Mushrooms | The Nutrition Source | Harvard T.H. Chan School of Public Health." The Nutrition Source, 19 Mar. 2020, https://www.hsph.harvard.edu/nutritionsource/food-features/mushrooms/.

"Mushrooms: Nutritional Value and Health Benefits." Medical and Health Information, Medical News Today, 6 Nov. 2019, https://www.medicalnewstoday.com/articles/278858.

Norris, Anna. "10 Bioluminescent Mushrooms That Glow in the Dark." Treehugger, Treehugger, 21 Apr. 2015, https://www.treehugger.com/bioluminescent-fungi-mushrooms-that-glow-in-the-dark-4868794.

Oder, Tom. "How to Identify Edible and Poisonous Wild Mushrooms." Treehugger, Treehugger, 30 Oct. 2013, https://www.treehugger.com/wild-mushrooms-what-to-eat-what-to-avoid-4864324.

"Otzi the Iceman: The Frozen Mummy's Mushrooms - Mossy Creek Mushrooms." Mossy Creek Mushrooms, https://www.facebook.com/mossycreekmushrooms/, 14 Mar. 2019, https://www.mossycreekmushrooms.com/blog-1/2019/03/14/otzi-the-iceman-the-frozen-mummys-mushrooms/.

"Poisonous Mushrooms: Facts, Myths, and Identification Information - Mushroom Appreciation." Mushroom Appreciation, 27 Feb. 2022, https://www.mushroom-appreciation.com/poisonous-mushrooms.html.

Robinson, Charles. "The Ethics of Mushroom Foraging — Fin + Forage." Fin + Forage, Fin + Forage, 19 Nov. 2020, https://finandforage.com/coastal-foraging/the-ethics-of-mushroom-foraging.

Salah, Mariam. "The NHBS Guide to Fungi Identification." NHBS - Wildlife, Ecology & Conservation, NHBS, 17 Sept. 2020, https://www.nhbs.com/blog/the-nhbs-guide-to-fungi-identification.

Sayner, Adam. "A Guide to All the Parts of a Mushroom - GroCycle." GroCycle, 26 Aug. 2021, https://grocycle.com/parts-of-a-mushroom/.

Shulman, Rachel. "Hunting for Wild Chicken of the Woods Mushrooms." Insteading, https://www.facebook.com/Insteading, 25 May 2010, https://insteading.com/blog/hunting-for-wild-chicken-mushrooms/.

Simpson, Michael. "How to Identify Edible Mushrooms (with Pictures) - WikiHow." WikiHow, wikiHow, 3 Dec. 2017, https://www.wikihow.com/Identify-Edible-Mushrooms.

"The Beginner's Guide to Foraging." Backpacker, 17 Sept. 2020, https://www.backpacker.com/skills/foraging/.

"The Case for Legal Foraging in America's National Parks." The Counter, https://www.facebook.com/thecountermedia/, 9 Jan. 2018, https://thecounter.org/the-case-for-legalizing-foraging-in-national-parks/.

"The Ethics of Mushroom Foraging — Fin + Forage." Fin + Forage, Fin + Forage, 19 Nov. 2020, https://finandforage.com/coastal-foraging/the-ethics-of-mushroom-foraging.

"The Forager's Dilemma -." Bay Nature, https://baynature.org/article/the-foragers-dilemma/.

"The Good, the Bad and the Tasty: The Many Roles of Mushrooms - PMC." PubMed Central (PMC), https://www.ncbi.nlm.nih.gov/pmc/articles/PMC5220184/.

"The Ultimate Functional Mushroom Guide: Reishi, Cordyceps, Chaga & Mor." Natural Force, Natural Force, 20 Jan. 2022, https://naturalforce.com/blogs/nutrition/medicinal-mushrooms#anchor3.

"The Ultimate Guide To Medicinal Mushrooms - FreshCap Mushrooms." FreshCap Mushrooms, https://learn.freshcap.com/tips/medicinal-mushrooms-guide/#how-to-take-mushrooms.

Thelwell, Kim. "Health and Economic Benefits of Mushrooms - The Borgen Project." The Borgen Project, https://www.facebook.com/borgenproject, 28 July 2020, https://borgenproject.org/benefits-of-mushrooms/.

"Three Amazing Medicinal Mushrooms - Forage London Guest Blog." Forage London and Beyond, 5 Apr. 2019, https://www.foragelondon.co.uk/three-amazing-medicinal-mushrooms%EF%BB%BF-you-can-collect-use-all-year-round-a-guest-blog-by-vicky-chown/.

"Tools and Resources for the Modern Forager." Modern Forager, https://facebook.com/modforager/, https://www.modern-forager.com/resources/.

"Top 5 Health Benefits of Mushrooms | BBC Good Food." BBC Good Food | Recipes and Cooking Tips - BBC Good Food, BBC Good Food, 23 May 2017, https://www.bbcgoodfood.com/howto/guide/health-benefits-mushrooms.

"Types of Parks for Mushroom Hunting [Ultimate Guide | 2021]." Mycelium Society | Mushroom Hunting and Cultivation, https://www.myceliumsociety.com/2021/06/16/types-of-parks-for-mushroom-hunting.html.

"Vancouver Island Mushrooms - Chanterelle Guide." Vancouver Island Mushrooms, https://www.westcoastforager.com/wild-edible-mushrooms/Chanterelle-Mushroom-Guide.

"What Is a Mushroom." Ministry of Forests Home Page, https://www.for.gov.bc.ca/hfp/publications/00029/mushwhat.htm.

"Where Do Mushrooms Come From? All Questions Answered - GroCycle." GroCycle, 6 Oct. 2021, https://grocycle.com/where-do-mushrooms-come-from.

Zhang, Sarah. "The Aftermath of a Deadly Mushroom Bloom in California - The Atlantic." The Atlantic, https://www.facebook.com/TheAtlantic/, 13 June 2017, https://www.theatlantic.com/science/archive/2017/06/death-cap-poisonings/530028/.

Brandenburg, W. E., & Ward, K. J. (2018). Mushroom poisoning epidemiology in the United States. *Mycologia*, *110*(4), 637–641. https://doi.org/10.1080/00275514.2018.1479561

Chung, M. J., Chung, C. K., Jeong, Y., & Ham, S. S. (2010). Anticancer activity of subfractions containing pure compounds of Chaga mushroom (Inonotus obliquus) extract in human cancer cells and in Balbc/c mice bearing Sarcoma-180 cells. Nutrition research and practice, 4(3), 177–182. https://doi.org/10.4162/nrp.2010.4.3.177

Norvell, Lorelei & Roger, Judy. The Oregon Cantharellus Study Project: Pacific Golden Chanterelle preliminary observations and productivity data (2016).

McKenna, Terrence. (1993). Food of the Gods: The Search for the Original Tree of Knowledge: A Radical History of Plants, Drugs, and Human Evolution. Bantam.

Stamets, Paul, and Heather Zwickey. "Medicinal Mushrooms: Ancient Remedies Meet Modern Science." Integrative medicine (Encinitas, Calif.) vol. 13,1 (2014): 46-7.

ALTA Language Services. (2022, May 17). Can mushrooms speak to each other? Scientists think it's possible. https://www.altalang.com/beyond-words/mushrooms-communicate/

Kelly, M. J. (2021, July 9). 100 communication quotes to remind you how powerful it is. Goalcast. https://www.goalcast.com/communication-quotes/

Made in the USA
Thornton, CO
08/22/24 17:43:29

45149857-d2e2-4150-899e-62a9e048d73cR01